TH COLONIZATION SOCIETY

An Avenue to Freedom?

Allan Yarema

University Press of America,® Inc.
Lanham · Boulder · New York · Toronto · Oxford

Copyright © 2006 by
University Press of America,® Inc.
4501 Forbes Boulevard
Suite 200
Lanham, Maryland 20706
UPA Acquisitions Department (301) 459-3366

PO Box 317
Oxford
OX2 9RU, UK

Library of Congress Control Number: 2005935325
ISBN 0-7618-3359-5 (paperback : alk. ppr.)

For Connie – the better half

Table of Contents

Preface and Acknowledgments

Even as the young American republic proudly viewed itself as a "city on a hill" and a beacon of democratic freedom to the world, it embraced an entrenched system of black slavery. James Madison decried this "peculiar institution" as a "sad blot on our free country," and Thomas Jefferson frankly acknowledged in his *Notes on the State of Virginia* that he believed the two races could never coexist. "Deep rooted prejudices" by the white population and "ten thousand recollections by the blacks," Jefferson insisted, would forever "divide us into parties, and produce convulsions which will probably never end but in the extermination of the one or the other race." This work focuses on a failed experiment known as the American Colonization Society.

Such men as Robert Finley, Elias Caldwell, and Francis Scott Key created the American Colonization Society in 1816 as a northern Christian and humanitarian outreach to free blacks. The initial goal of the Society was colonizing free blacks in Africa. Madison gladly welcomed the birth of this effort and worked actively with it at both state and national levels. He understood that one of the chief obstacles which southern slaveholders faced was the question of the status of the slaves once their bondage ended, and Madison hoped that the Society would provide the answer and mechanism to end slavery. Transporting free blacks outside the United States seemed wisest to both Madison and Jefferson and other prominent slaveholders who also embraced colonization. Henry Clay added his stature to the organization and eventually, like Madison, took command of the movement as its national president. Eminent Americans from both slave and free states placed their efforts and faith in this movement which embodied "the plans, hopes, and achievements of men, inspired by many motives, who sought to rid the country of an unwanted race."

This study explores the origin, purpose, growth, and ultimate failure of the American Colonization Society in the early nineteenth century. The Society, organized and supported by prominent humanitarians and sympathetic politicians, became a popular social movement in both the North and the South. Support rose in the 1820s and early 1830s, but waned in the later 1830s and 1840s because of radical abolitionists' attacks. Yet it revived in the 1850s as the issue of slavery increasingly polarized the nation. For many people throughout the republic who opposed political and economic equality for free blacks, African colonization was a satisfactory compromise between opposing and hostile forces fighting for either the preservation of slavery or its immediate demise.

The colonization movement ultimately failed for a variety of reasons, in both its initial goal of colonizing free blacks in Africa and in its later objective of encouraging voluntary emancipation. The prohibitive expenses involved in transporting and resettling immigrants to Africa at length rendered the project impractical. Beyond this, most free blacks proved unwilling recruits to the cause of resettlement. They considered the United States their home and wished only to improve their condition in the land of their birth. Colonization, moreover, provoked radical abolitionist opposition on the grounds of racism. Firebrand abolitionists insisted that the Society's propaganda, branding free blacks as inferior and incapable of citizenship, lowered rather than elevated blacks and served only to increase prejudice and hatred. At the same time radical abolitionists relentlessly attacked the Society as a conspiracy designed to strengthen rather than diminish slavery. Furthermore, most in the Deep South rejected the colonization scheme as a threat to the cornerstone of the region's socio-economic system. As cotton production became, through time, extraordinarily profitable for the Deep South, this unprecedented wealth hinged upon a large and unfree labor force.

Arrayed against such formidable and implacable foes, colonization gained little effective credence as a viable resolution to the incendiary issue of slavery. Well-meaning and good-intentioned supporters advocated and nurtured the colonization scheme through four decades, even launching several African ventures. But in the end the broad-based popular endorsement essential to the success of any such pivotal movement in a democracy, never materialized. Instead, the republic plunged itself into a horrific civil war–the issue would be decided by blood.

My work was facilitated by many people. In particular I am grateful to Professor Ralph Goodwin who introduced me to American history and to the American Colonization Society. I am also indebted to Professor John Robinson who carefully edited my manuscript and offered valuable suggestions. Finally, my wife Connie worked with me from beginning to end, and I am grateful for her constant help and patience.

Abilene, Texas
July 16, 2005

Chapter 1
Slavery and Free Blacks: An American Dilemma

The American Revolution, deriving its rationale from the dictum that "all men are created equal," gave birth, paradoxically, to a republic marked by the institution of slavery. The new nation, pledging a commitment to individual freedom and human rights, continued to subjugate most of its black people to slavery until a bloody sectional conflict brought that practice to a violent end in 1865. In the years before the dilemma exploded into civil war, Americans proposed a variety of solutions to the problem, among them a failed experiment beginning with the colonization of free blacks and ending in gradual emancipation.

African blacks were introduced into Jamestown by Dutch shippers as forced laborers or indentured servants as early 1619. Whatever the original status of these black workers, well before 1700 blacks had become servants for life under the laws of Maryland, Virginia, and South Carolina.[1] The system of chattel slavery, which eventually spread to all the English colonies in America, crystallized into a legal and perpetual institution.

At the end of the American Revolution, the southern states held the greatest concentrations of slaves because of the intensive labor required for such productive crops as tobacco, rice, and indigo. The black population remained relatively sparse in the northern states where slavery offered few real economic advantages, since an economy based on commerce, small-scale farming, and handcrafted industries offered little advantage to forced labor. White indentured servants and free laborers satisfied the needs of farmers who did not need workers all year round and provided a reliable work force for the new manufacturing establishments.

Emancipation, therefore, proved neither difficult nor costly in the North. The abolition of slavery in the North, however, "should not be considered simply on the grounds of profits and losses, climate, or geography." The same principals used to justify the American Revolution were also extended to slavery. Many conscientious Americans were troubled by the inconsistency of opposing what they perceived as British tyranny with the practice and acceptance of slavery. Religious groups like the Quakers played an active role in abolishing slavery.[2]

The Vermont constitution outlawed slavery in 1777, while New Hampshire and Massachusetts later ended the practice through judicial decisions. In 1780 the Pennsylvania legislature passed the first act for gradual emancipation, decreeing that the children of slaves be set free on their twenty-eighth birthdays. Rhode Island, Connecticut, and New York enacted similar legislation, and in 1804 New Jersey also enacted gradual emancipation.[3]

Yet the end of slavery brought only limited freedom for blacks since they continued to be systematically denied the full rights and privileges of citizenship. Theoretically free in the North, blacks endured blatant discrimination and treatment as a supposedly inferior race. Laws or court decisions could not erase the racism clouding the minds of most white Americans who dismissed blacks as inferior and incapable of being assimilated into American society or politics. Free blacks were denied the right to vote or serve on juries or in the militia. Negrophobia kept blacks from most trades and occupations and restricted them to menial employment. Free blacks were also excluded throughout the country from hotels, inns, taverns, schools, and residential districts. Even cemeteries denied them burial.[4]

Many state legislatures also proscribed residency for free blacks. Delaware in 1811 prohibited residency to free blacks and mulattoes, and in the District of Columbia, free blacks had to prove their freedom by documentary evidence or be sold into slavery. Ohio's first legislature required free blacks and mulattoes who wished to reside in the state to present certificates of freedom, documents essential for employment. New states carved out of the Northwest Territory either barred free blacks or demanded certificates of freedom as prerequisites to residency. In addition, free blacks posted bonds ranging from $500 to $1,000, which requirement effectively barred most. Northern states commonly enacted similar laws. Legislation to limit free blacks was passed in Illinois in 1819, 1829, and 1853; Indiana in 1831 and 1852; Ohio in 1804 and

1807; and the Oregon Territory in 1849. Residents hiring free blacks without certificates of freedom were subject to fines.[5]

Rather than acknowledge the racism which prompted such laws and limitations, whites claimed that if the population of free blacks grew, then poverty and crime must also increase. Free blacks, it was widely asserted, inflated public costs for poor relief and law enforcement. Beyond this, white laborers feared job competition from free blacks willing to work for lower wages, while others expressed alarm that free blacks might demand political and social equality. Despite the fact that northern states were enacting or had already adopted laws abolishing slavery, most white Americans opposed equal political and economic rights for free blacks.[6]

For many whites, especially those whose humanitarian and religious views made them more sympathetic to the black man's condition, this produced a social and moral quandary. They assumed that assimilation of the two races was impossible, at least for the foreseeable future, yet their principles mitigated against the prejudicial treatment accorded free blacks. The only humane and just solution for many seemed to lie in providing a way to resettle free blacks outside the United States.

As early as 1714 a proposal to return blacks to Africa appeared in an obscure pamphlet entitled *American Defense of the Christian Golden Rule*. The author suggested that emancipated blacks be resettled in Africa to serve as missionaries. Masters, voluntarily, rather than by force of law, should set their slaves free to return "to their own country," and money could be solicited from slave owners or other interested persons to defray the costs of repatriation. Nothing further is known about this proposal or who its author was.[7] Thus in the early colonial period some Americans had already given serious consideration to deporting freed blacks to Africa.

Such theorists took no practical steps to carry out this idea, but a similar plan would be proposed on August 31, 1773 on the eve of the revolutionary crisis. Samuel D. Hopkins, minister of the First Congregational Church in Newport, Rhode Island, with help from Ezra Stiles, fellow cleric at the Second Congregational Church in Newport, launched a circular soliciting funds for the training of two ex-slaves, Bristo Yamma and John Quamine, to be sent as missionaries to Africa. They collected enough money, largely from New England, to support Yamma and Quamine at Princeton College to receive the necessary religious training for their missionary undertaking, and in 1776 Hopkins sent out a second circular requesting further financial aid for this African mission. The

War of Independence, however, cut off all contributions, and this missionary endeavor ended. Quamine died in battle on board a privateer in 1779, and Yamma ended his days as a free laborer in North Carolina. Hopkins is considered the father of the scheme to send free blacks back to Africa.[8]

Although the War of Independence blocked Hopkins' African missionary venture, it stirred in him new and larger ideas. Together with many of the revolutionary generation, Hopkins was disturbed by the glaring contradiction between the existence of slavery and the professed ideals of the new nation. Hopkins worried particularly about the brutalities of the slave trade and saw slavery as a blemish on America's image as the standard-bearer of civil and religious liberty. In proposing that all slaves be set free and transported to Africa, he foresaw multiple benefits: Christianity and civilization would expand, commercial routes with new markets would be created, the slave trade would eventually cease, and blacks could at last enjoy true social equality in their "native land." Hopkins' visionary blueprint for such a large-scale resettlement effort attracted little support at this time because of the tremendous costs entailed, but his arguments did stimulate an interest that would later produce more pragmatic efforts to resettle free blacks in Africa. Others would keep this idea alive.

Beyond a coterie of New England ministers, some southerners, sensitive to the incompatibility of their "peculiar institution" with Enlightenment ideals and notions of Christian brotherhood, found the concept attractive. To such men as Thomas Jefferson, deportation offered the only means of achieving gradual emancipation without inviting race war and social anarchy. With Jefferson as probably one of the most influential advocates of black deportation, the Virginia legislature in 1776 appointed a committee to revise and codify the laws of Virginia and to propose a general plan for emancipating slaves. The committee, chosen by the General Assembly, included Thomas Jefferson, George Wythe, and Edmund Pendleton. Their report, submitted to the General Assembly in June 1779, recommended an amendment to Virginia's constitution freeing the children of slaves at the age of twenty-one for males and at eighteen for females. Prior to emancipation, children were to remain with their parents, learning the skills necessary to make them self-sufficient. Later they would be sent, at public expense, to some territory outside the United States.[9]

Jefferson later included the text of this proposal for gradual emancipation in Virginia and resettlement of the freed blacks in his *Notes on the*

State of Virginia, published in 1787. Jefferson argued that deportation was necessary because of strong antagonisms on the part of both races. The two races, he held, could never coexist peacefully on terms of equality. "Deep rooted prejudices entertained by the whites; ten thousand recollections by the blacks; the real distinctions which nature had made; and many other circumstances," Jefferson insisted, "will divide us into parties, and produce convulsions which will probably never end but in the extermination of the one or the other race."[10] Such a fearsome prospect demanded extraordinary measures.

Some years later, in a letter to a friend in 1811, Jefferson indicated that he had always thought that a plan to gradually deport blacks would benefit both the white and the black populations. As president, he had explored in vain the possibility of colonizing freed American slaves in the British-sponsored African settlement of Sierra Leone, as well as in South America. Now as a private citizen, Jefferson supported the suggestion that the United States itself should undertake to plant a colony for free blacks on the western coast of Africa. The expense of such a venture might be defrayed, he proposed, by capitalizing on the commercial advantages such a settlement would offer to American manufacturers and shippers.[11] Yet despite his personal enthusiasm, Jefferson expressed doubt that the national mind was ready for such an endeavor.

Thirteen years later, shortly before his death, Jefferson still urged, privately, the feasibility of such an African settlement. Two major objectives, he argued, would be achieved by sending the whole black population gradually to Africa. First, resettled American blacks would transmit the blessing of art, civilization, and science to Africa. "We shall in the long run," Jefferson rationalized, "have rendered [American slaves] perhaps more good than evil." Second, colonized blacks would for the first time experience freedom and independence under the care and protection of the United States government. Jefferson believed that this plan would not only promote the happiness and well-being of blacks, but also of the whites remaining in America.[12]

Jefferson, estimating a population of approximately one and a half million black slaves in the country, valued each slave at roughly two hundred dollars. The cost of emancipation, thus, would total some six hundred million dollars. In addition, three hundred million dollars would be needed to cover the expenses of transportation, food, clothing, and implements. Jefferson recommended a plan for incremental resettlement stretching over twenty-five years. The cost of such a venture, he acknowledged, would lessen its appeal, so as an alternative he recommended the plan he had proposed earlier in *Notes on the State of Virginia*, in which all newborn slaves would be freed but remain in their mothers' care, until old enough to be transported. Jefferson naïvely hoped that most slave owners would free their newborn slaves without remuneration in order to bring slavery gradually to an end, thus eliminating six hundred million dollars otherwise required for emancipation. Since the slave owner would incur the cost of maintaining the child while he remained with his mother, only the later costs for transportation and resettlement need become a public obligation. Funds for this purpose, Jefferson suggested, might come from the sale of public lands. As the emancipated young left the country each year, the old slaves remaining would gradually die, thus ending slavery.[13] Such a scheme, of course, roused no interest among slaveholders.

Despite such early indications of American interest in colonization, the British seized the initiative by establishing a settlement of former slaves in Africa. Late in the eighteenth century Granville Sharp, a pioneer abolitionist, joined a group of wealthy English philanthropists, to create a relief committee for poor blacks living in London whom the British army had rescued during the American War of Independence. The committee eventually adopted a plan to resettle poor blacks in western Africa. Backed by Sharp and his associates, Captain Tom Taylor of the British Navy purchased land from King Tom, a Temme subchief, and established a beachhead in Sierra Leone on the African coast in 1787, thus laying the foundation of the proposed settlement. But because of native hostilities, mass desertions, and a ruinous fever, the fledging colony disbanded in 1789.

Three years later Sharp and opponents of the slave trade, such as William Wilberforce, revived the effort when the Sierra Leone Company planted a new colony called Freetown. With free blacks coming also from Nova Scotia and Jamaica, the colony became permanent. Then in 1808 the company was forced by near bankruptcy to surrender ownership of the settlement to the British government which had abolished the slave trade in 1807. From that point forward the British used Sierra Leone as a naval base for operations against the slave trade and as a station to return recaptured slaves. Originally, Sierra Leone (Lion Mountain) received its name from Portuguese explorers in the 15th century, and by the 16th century Europeans were purchasing slaves from it. The British Parliament commissioned Henry Smeathman, a naturalist, to explore its potential as a possible convict settlement. Parliament, however, eventually rejected the plan because of the possibility of native hostility and of the fear that it would interfere with Britain's trading routes in the area. Consequently, Smeathman contacted the committee for poor relief of blacks, proposing a scheme to conduct poor blacks from London to Sierra Leone for a fee. Sierra Leone would also provide a base for trade with the interior of Africa. This prospect appealed to Sharp and Wilberforce and other British philanthropist and abolitionist merchants, bankers, and shippers. The scheme for Sierra Leone included economic and commercial purposes, as well as Christian and humanitarian. American African colonization would result from similar motives.[14] Sierra Leone would become a model that many Americans hoped the United States would follow.

American advocates of black resettlement demonstrated interest in areas apart from Africa as possible sites of colonization. Thomas Branagan, a Pennsylvania Quaker and former slave trader, suggested in 1805 a settlement on the western side of the Allegheny Mountains. Branagan's pamphlet, *Serious Remonstrances, Addressed to the Citizens of the Northern States and their Representatives*, reiterated some of Jefferson's proposals for emancipating and resettling Virginia's slave population, but Branagan tailored his plea to appeal to white self-interest. Free blacks should be removed, he argued, because they took away employment from the white laborers, hindered immigration from Europe, and posed a constant danger to the safety of society. He suggested that territory in the newly acquired Louisiana Purchase be set aside for black settlement. Each black who paid his own way to the settlement would be offered free land in the region which would be supervised by a governor and the necessary judges and magistrates appointed by the president.[15] Branagan's plan attracted no practical support in a Congress deeply reluctant to interfere with the domestic institutions of the separate states.

Regardless of the lack of any national programs, several states had already taken steps to promote the removal of free blacks. Complex motives prompted Negro exclusion. Unlike the colonization schemes proposed by New England ministers and Thomas Jefferson, Negro exclusion was, in the South, ordinarily inspired less by the desire to encourage gradual emancipation than to buttress the institution of slavery by banishing freed slaves. A substantial free black presence was seen as a potent source of incitement to servile insurrection. From colonial days laws had been passed requiring the deportation of blacks convicted of crime. As early as 1691 Virginia imposed such a requirement, as well as stipulating that any emancipated slave must leave the colony within six months at the former owner's expense. If the freed black was still in the colony after this time limit, the owner was fined ten pounds to defray the cost of deporting the freed slave.[16]

Other colonies also imposed such requirements for black deportation. After 1705 any black convicted in Pennsylvania for attempted rape, robbery, or theft was to be deported after being whipped and branded. If the convicted was a slave, the owner bore the expense of transportation; a free black convicted of such crimes must leave at his own expense.[17]

Nearly one hundred years later, the Virginia General Assembly in 1800 requested the governor to write the President of the United States suggesting a plan for establishing a penal colony for blacks beyond the limits of Virginia. Virginia offered to buy the necessary land to which all persons, notably blacks, considered "obnoxious" and "dangerous" to the stability of society could be removed.[18] Then Governor James Monroe wrote President Jefferson proposing such a penal colony for persons convicted of high crimes and misdemeanors. He explained that the Gabriel slave revolt of 1800 had prompted the legislature's resolution. The only persons to be deported to the penal colony would be those slaves who took part in the revolt. Gabriel Prosser with several hundred slaves planned to march upon Richmond and capture the governor. Gabriel's plan was discovered; consequently, Governor Monroe suppressed this slave uprising near Richmond, in August, 1800. Although the revolt was easily put down, the white population near Richmond went into a state of hysteria.[19] Monroe asked whether a tract of land in the western territory of the United States could be purchased by Virginia for this purpose. This request, he acknowledged, clearly involved "the future peace, tranquility, and happiness of the good people of the Commonwealth." Monroe said nothing about non-criminal free blacks or slaves being considered for deportation, but he did call slavery "an existing evil" inflicted upon this generation from the colonial past.[20]

In reply Jefferson acknowledged that he understood the proposed penal settlement was not directed against the common criminal, but rather, against those involved in slave conspiracies and insurrections. Jefferson could not recommend purchasing land in or near the territory of the United States because such an area might eventually become part of the Union. The West Indies, in particular Santo Domingo, he believed would have more reasonable possibilities. Both locales had people of the same race; the climate also would be more suitable. Africa might be considered if no other territory could be found, but Jefferson worried that the high cost of transportation across the Atlantic could make this unfeasible.[21] He indicated that when the Virginia legislature had more definite plans, he would contact the proper foreign authorities.

On January 16, 1802, the Virginia General Assembly passed a second resolution outlining in more detail its plan for a penal settlement outside the state. The resolution made it clear that this proposed colony was for persons convicted not for ordinary crimes, but for slave conspiracy and insurrection. The real purpose apparently reached more broadly than this. It was suggested additionally that free blacks, mulattoes, and those who might be emancipated in the future could also be resettled in such a colony and suggested Africa as a possible site.[22] Jefferson then wrote Rufus King, the United States minister to Great Britain, instructing him to make inquiries of the British government for permission to send American free blacks to Sierra Leone.[23] Eventually the British rejected the request, concluding, that the United States was only attempting to rid itself of troublesome blacks.

Almost two years later President Jefferson reopened the issue of relocating free blacks with Governor John Page of Virginia. By this time the situation had changed significantly, especially in the wake of the successful slave uprising in Santo Domingo. Obviously this site would no longer be suitable for Virginia's purpose. As a possible alternative, Jefferson suggested the lands of Louisiana, which had only recently been purchased from France.[24] In response the Virginia General Assembly formally urged the state's senators and representatives in Congress to do what they could to obtain a portion of Louisiana for possible settlement. The resolution urged Virginia's senators and representatives to "exert their best possible efforts for the purpose of obtaining from the General Government a competent portion of territory, in the country of Louisiana, to be appropriated to the residence of such people of colour as have been or shall be emancipated in Virginia, or may hereafter become dangerous to the public safety."[25] Whatever efforts Virginia's spokesmen in Congress may have made, no further action was taken. The nation's preoccupation with diplomatic troubles growing out of the Napoleonic war retarded any possible movement in this direction.

A few tumultuous years later in the aftermath of the War of 1812, a new spirit of nationalism swept over the United States. The war seemed to demonstrate the young republic's capability of protecting its national interests against a power such as Great Britain. Americans now developed new confidence in themselves and a "renewed sense of a common national experience," as enthusiasm grew for new policies such as a protective tariff, a new national bank, and a system of roads and canals to bind the different sections of the country together economically.[26]

Almost simultaneously a new wave of religious enthusiasm, the "second Great Awakening," reflected the buoyant new hopes as well as certain new fears of the American people. As revivals spread throughout different communities, a new Christian benevolent consciousness emerged. Among those deeply touched was Samuel Hopkins of the First Congregational Church in Newport, Rhode Island. Hopkins, as already noted, was a committed advocate of black resettlement. His social concerns sprang from the popular new theological tenet of "disinterested benevolence," the conception that man's true moral character demanded performing good deeds free of any personal benefit. With so many others in this era, Hopkins optimistically believed that society could be changed and perfected in preparation for the long-awaited millennial reign of God upon earth. But first, to open the way for this dazzling future, society required reformation—thus the need for benevolent associations, voluntary organizations of dedicated Christians working to improve the lot of their fellow men. The goal was to transform society through organized social action into a "homogeneous Protestant, Bible reading, industrious society."[27]

Although not typical of most Americans in this era, the "benevolent society" movement reflected the intensity of commitment to social concerns by a comparatively small group.[28] A host of new private associations dedicated to a broad spectrum of religious and social uplift sprang into existence. These benevolent societies included the American Sunday School Union, the American Tract Society, the American Peace Society, the American Temperance Union, the American Education Society, the American Board of Commissioners for Foreign Missions, the American Home Missionary Society, the American Seamen's Friend Society, and the American Society for Meliorating the Condition of the Jews.[29]

Benevolent societies often stood in the forefront of efforts on behalf of the nation's most exploited under class, the free blacks. Among supporters of justice and equal opportunity for free blacks was Robert Finley, a retired Presbyterian minister of Baskingridge, New Jersey. Finley at first expressed concern over free blacks in his neighborhood who could not read the religious tracts they were given. He then committed himself to funding a benevolent society devoted to improving the condition of free blacks. His interest stretched beyond promoting literacy. Equality, he grew convinced, would remain an impossible goal for blacks as long as they lived among whites. By 1815 Finley came to believe that the most practical way to improve the condition of free blacks was through resettlement in a special colony on some part of the western coast of Africa. He argued that colonization would benefit both the North and South. In the North the free black population was "unfavorable to our industry and morals," and by removing them, pauperism and immorality would be reduced thus benefiting society. Resettlement would also benefit the South by providing a way to voluntarily and gradually end slavery, thus relieving southerners' fears that emancipation was reckless and dangerous.[30] Finley envisioned three benefits of resettlement: "We should be clear of them," Finley wrote frankly; "we should send to Africa a population partly civilized and Christianized, for its benefits—our blacks themselves would be put in a better situation."[31] Notwithstanding his perhaps genuine concern for blacks' welfare, Finley's views on colonization reflected a paradox central to the movement. On the one hand it was founded on the inherently racist assumption that blacks were incapable of assimilation into white society; on the other hand, the movement relied upon the same "inassimilable" people to carry civilization and Christianity to Africa. Colonizationists explained this paradox by arguing that while blacks could not be totally assimilated into white society, they were nevertheless sufficiently civilized and Christianized to benefit their even more backward kinsmen in Africa.

In November, 1816 Finley laid out his proposal for a colonization society to a small gathering of townspeople, professors, and students at Princeton, New Jersey. He suggested that the new society be located in Washington D.C. where it would be best placed to influence Congress. The organization would begin as a private endeavor, but once the colony had been established, the federal government must assume the burden of maintaining it. Only the nation as a whole could muster the economic resources to sustain such a venture, so financial help from Congress would be essential for the enterprise's success.[32] With his plan endorsed by the Princeton meeting, Finley left for Washington in December, 1816 to recruit help in establishing the proposed society. Finley was confident: "I know this scheme is from God."[33] That divine mission intended to promote an exodus purging America of its black population.

NOTES

1. Oscar and Mary F. Handlin, "Origins of the Southern Labor System," *William and Mary Quarterly* 7 (April 1950): 199-222; Winthrop D. Jordan, *White Over Black: American Attitudes Toward the Negro, 1550-1812* (Chapel Hill: University of North Carolina Press, 1968), 44-98.

2. Frederic Bancroft, "The Early Antislavery Movement and African Colonization," in *Fredric Bancroft, Historian: With an Introduction By Allan Nevins and Three Hitherto Unpublished Essays on the Colonization of American Negroes from 1801 to 1865 By Fredric Bancroft*, ed. Jacob E. Cooke (Norman: University of Oklahoma Press, 1957), 147-148; Leon F. Litwack, *North of Slavery: The Negro in the Free States 1790-1860*, (Chicago: The University of Chicago Press, 1961), 3-15.

3. Robert William Fogel, *Without Consent or Contract: The Rise and Fall of American Slavery* (New York: W. W. Norton, 1989), 246; Litwack, *North of Slavery*, 3.

4. John Bach McMaster, *A History of the United States, From Revolution to the Civil War* (New York: D. Appleton and Company, 1921), 5:185-186; Litwack, *North of Slavery*, 15-16.

5. McMaster, *History of the United States*, 5:187; Litwack, *North of Slavery*, 66-74.

6. Henry N. Sherwood, "Early Deportation Projects," *Mississippi Valley Historical Review* 2 (March 1916): 486.

7. Mary Stoughton Locke, *Anti-Slavery in American from the Introduction of African Slaves to the Prohibition of the Slave Trade, 1619-1808* (Boston: Radcliffe College, 1901; reprinted Gloucester: Peter Smith, 1865), 30.

8. Leonard I. Sweet, *Black Images of America, 1784-1870* (New York: W.W. Norton and Company, Inc., 1976), 23-24; Sherwood, "Early Deportation Projects," 497-500; Archibald Alexander, *A History of Colonization of the Western Coast of Africa,* 2nd ed. (Freeport: Books For Library Press, 1971; reprint, Philadelphia: William S. Martien, 1849), 63.

9. Thomas Jefferson, "Notes on the State of Virginia," *The Portable Thomas Jefferson*, Merrill D. Peterson, ed. (New York: Penguin Books, 1975), 185-186.

10. *Ibid.*

11. Jefferson to John Lynch, January 21, 1811, in *Writings of Jefferson*, Paul Leicester Ford, ed. (New York: G. P. Putnam's Sons, 1898) 8:303-304.

12. Jefferson of Jared Sparks, February 4, 1824, *Ibid.*, 10:289-290.

13. *Ibid.*, 291-293.

14. James W. St. G. Walker, *The Black Loyalists: The Search for a Promised Land in Nova Scotia and Sierra Leone 1783-1870* (New York: Africana Publishing Company and Dalhousie University Press, 1976), 96-107; A. P. Kup, *Sierra Leone: A Concise History* (New York: St. Martin's Press, 1875), 115-123; Francis A. J. Utting, *The Story of Sierra Leone* (Hallandale: New World

Book Manufacturing, 1931; reprint, Freeport: Books for Libraries Press, 1971), 82-96; John Peterson, *Province of Freedom: A History of Sierra Leone 1787-1870* (Evanston, Northwestern University Press, 1969), 18-44; Philip J. Staudenraus, *The African Colonization Movement, 1816-1865*, (New York: Columbia University Press, 1961), 8-9.

15. Sherwood, "Early Deportation Projects," 495-496.

16. *Ibid.*, 484-485.

17. *Ibid.*

18. Resolution of the House of Delegates, December 31, 1800, in Alexander, *History of Colonization*, 63.

19. Marshall Smelser, *The Democratic Republic, 1801-1815* (New York: Harper and Row, 1968), 42.

20. Monroe to Thomas Jefferson, June 15, 1801, in *The Writings of James Monroe*, Stanislaus Murry Hamilton, ed. (New York: G. P. Putnam's Sons, 1900), 3:292-295.

21. Jefferson to Monroe, November 24, 1810, in Ford, Writings of Jefferson, 8:103-106.

22. Resolution from Virginia's General Assembly, January 16, 1802, in Alexander, *History of Colonization*, 69 -70.

23. Jefferson to Rufus King, July 13, 1802, in Ford, *Writings of Jefferson*, 8:161-163.

24. Jefferson to Governor John Page, December 23, 1803, in *The Writings of Jefferson*, Albert Bergh, ed. (Washington: The Thomas Jefferson Memorial Association, 1905), 19:138.

25. Resolution of the Virginia General Assembly, December 3, 1804, in Alexander, *History of Colonization*, 71-72.

26. George Dangerfield, *The Awakening of American Nationalism, 1815-1828*, (New York: Harper and Row, 1965), 4; Smelser, *Democratic Republic*, 324.

27. Staudenraus, *African Colonization*, 12-15.

28. Robert V. Remini, *The Revolutionary Age of Andrew Jackson* (New York: Harper & Row, 1987), 17.

29. Edward Pessen, *Jacksonian America: Society, Personality, and Politics* (Urbana: University of Illinois Press, 1985), 67-75.

30. Staudenraus, *African Colonization*, 20.

31. Finley to John P. Mumford, February 14, 1816, in Isaac V. Brown, *Biography of the Rev. Robert Finley* (Philadelphia: John W. Moore, 1857; reprint, New York: Arno Press and The New York Times, 1969), 99-100.

32. *Ibid.*, 19-22.

33. "American Colonization Society," *The African Repository and Colonial Journal* 1 (March 1825): 1-4; Charles Marrow Wilson, *Liberia: Black Africa in Microcosm* (New York: Harper and Row, 1971), 6.

Chapter 2
A Black-Free America

The American Colonization Society was formed initially as a northern Christian and humanitarian organization to resettle free blacks in Africa as seen by its founders and promoters, Robert Finley, Elias Caldwell, and Francis Scott Key. Leaders and supporters would eventually come from the ranks of slave owners themselves, such as James Madison, Henry Clay, and John Randolph. By focusing its goal on resettling free blacks to Africa, the Society brought together friends and enemies of slavery. It would begin as a private endeavor, but once a colony had been established to demonstrate the concept's feasibility, the federal government would assume the burden of maintaining it. To raise both funds and build public support for colonization, early state and local auxiliaries flourished in Virginia, Maryland, Georgia, and North and South Carolina. Auxiliaries were also founded in northern cities such as Boston, New Haven, Hartford, Providence, Philadelphia, New York City, and Baltimore, along with many church organizations endorsing and financially supporting the movement. As tensions heightened over the slavery issue, voluntary and gradual emancipation also became a goal for the advocates of colonization.

Armed with the endorsement of the Princeton meeting of December, 1816, Robert Finley quickly found the help he needed in Washington for establishing the national society he envisioned for promoting a "truly Christian" solution to the problem of free blacks in a segregated society. Elias Caldwell, Finley's brother-in-law, practiced law and served as clerk of the Supreme Court between 1800 and 1824. Through these activities Caldwell came to know most of the prominent lawyers and politicians who moved in the capital's circles, such as Henry Clay, Daniel Webster, John Calhoun, and General Lafayette. These men often dined at his table. After the British burned the capitol building in 1814, the Supreme Court met in his house until the new capitol was rebuilt. Among others, Caldwell recruited the "Star Spangled Banner's" composer, Francis Scott Key, then a successful Washington lawyer, to help form this new society.[1] Key also served as vice-president of the American Bible Society and helped manage the American Sunday School Union. Such spokesmen connected the identity of reform with the emerging spirit of American nationalism. Together, Finley, Caldwell, and Key worked to raise public support for a colonization society, but much work needed to be done before their hopes could become reality.

Finley issued a pamphlet urging the colonization plan and distributed it among congressmen and senators, while Caldwell and Key wrote articles championing the cause in the *Daily National Intelligencer*. After these three men secured enough names to assure a respectable showing of support, they planned a meeting at the Davies Hotel for December 21, 1816. Caldwell and Key persuaded Bushrod Washington, George Washington's nephew and veteran Supreme Court Justice, Henry Clay, Speaker of the House, and the redoubtable John Randolph of Roanoke to support the meeting. An advertisement in the *Intelligencer* invited all interested persons living in Washington, Georgetown, Alexandria, Baltimore, Annapolis, and Fredericksburg to the meeting.[2]

Bushrod Washington was to chair the meeting, but was unable to attend. Henry Clay, acting as temporary chairman in Justice Washington's absence, called the meeting to order and spoke briefly, proposing to form a society for colonizing free blacks.[3] He pointed out that although free blacks were not slaves, they did not enjoy the freedoms accorded white people in American society. This condition, reinforced by the deep-seated prejudice so widely shared throughout the country, rendered it impossible for free blacks to integrate into the dominant white society. Consequently, colonization offered the only realistic option for free blacks. Clay pointed to Sierra Leone as an example of a successful colonization project:

> We have their experience before us, and can there be a nobler cause than that which, while it proposes to rid our country of a useless and pernicious, if not dangerous portion of its population, contemplates the spreading of arts of civilized life, and the possible redemption of ignorance and barbarism of a benighted portion of the globe.[4]

Clay, himself a slave owner, strongly emphasized that the proposed society would work only with free blacks and not with the slave population.

Abolition, Clay insisted, must not be associated with the aims of colonization.

Elias Caldwell then addressed the gathering, declaring that America could not continue upholding civil liberties while depriving a part of its population of these same liberties. Caldwell and other supporters of colonizing free blacks seemed convinced that the white man's racial attitudes could never be changed. James Madison, for example, stated that blacks could never be accepted as equals because of "the prejudices of the Whites, prejudices which proceeding principally from the difference of colour must be considered as permanent and insuperable." Most supporters of colonization opposed any legislation giving free blacks the right to vote and supported racial restrictions. No amount of education or economic independence would soften the racist attitudes of whites against blacks. Therefore, according to the colonizationists, resettling free blacks outside the United States was both humane and just. Colonizing free blacks seemed a reasonable and viable option.[5] The western coast of Africa, Caldwell suggested, would be the best place to colonize free blacks since from there they could spread Christianity throughout the continent. Would free blacks be willing to participate in African colonization? The opportunity to enjoy equality and civil rights in a new land of their own should provide all the incentive needed. After all, Caldwell pointed out, this was how the United States itself had been established.[6]

John Randolph, also a slave owner, agreed with Clay that the proposed association to colonize free blacks must not, in any way, challenge the institution of slavery itself. He suggested, however, that every slaveholder ought to be interested in the association since many slaveholders believed that the presence of free blacks created a dangerous source of discontent among slaves. Free blacks also offered convenient channels through which slaves passed stolen goods. Colonizing free blacks would thereby diminish multiple threats to slaveholders.

This first meeting generated three resolutions. The first established an association to collect information and form a plan for colonizing free blacks, with their consent, in Africa or wherever Congress might choose. A second resolution created a committee instructed to present a memorial to Congress urging that a colonization project be adopted officially. The third resolution authorized another committee which should draw up a constitution and rules for the society itself.

From the very beginning, the new Society's goal focused ostensibly on resettling free blacks in Africa. This limited definition of the Society's objective temporarily brought together friends and enemies of slavery in a single-issue organization. Proponents of slavery could find in the project a safeguard for the "peculiar institution." Thus local colonization societies briefly flourished in Georgia and the Carolinas in 1817-1818.[7] The disavowal of emancipation goals by such slaveholders as Henry Clay and John Randolph was clearly designed to avoid alienating southern slaveholding interests. As the Great Compromiser, Clay could be expected to seek a resolution of the American dilemma which would not provoke sectional animosities or social anarchy.

Clay would become one of the strongest proponents of African colonization. Once the Society was formed, he continued to be an active member, spoke on its behalf, served as one of its vice-presidents and then, in 1836, its president. Clay owned as many as fifty slaves, and shortly before his death counted thirty-three slaves among his holdings. Clay bequeathed these to his heirs with the stipulation that all children born from these bondsmen be emancipated (the males at age twenty-eight and the females at twenty-five) and transported to western Africa. Like Clay, John Randolph also owned a large number of slaves and freed them through his will, which included provisions for their transportation and resettlement in Ohio.[8]

Despite the heterogeneous backgrounds of those who led the intersectional alliance of colonizationists, all agreed on the need for social reform. Finley and Caldwell feared an increase of indigence, illiteracy, and secularization among free blacks, while Clay and Randolph viewed free blacks as a threat to republican virtues. Such a "depressed" and "backward" population, they argued, simply lacked the talent and inclination to develop into good citizens. The Colonization Society attracted support from those whose motives ranged from Christian benevolence to concerns for republican purity. Men with diverse views worked together to articulate a program that they believed offered the best hope for alleviating the national moral and social ills which they attributed to an increasing free black presence.[9]

The new Society's second meeting convened on December 28, 1816 in the hall of the House of Representatives. The gathering adopted a constitution composed of ten articles and renamed itself "The American Society for colonizing the free people of Color of the United States." Eventually this would be shortened to the American Colonization Society. The initial title reflected the object of the Society: to resettle free blacks in Africa, with their consent and in cooperation with the national government. Chosen to direct the organization were a president, thirteen

vice-presidents, a secretary, a treasurer, a recorder, and a board of managers. The board of managers, elected annually by the Society's members, conducted the business and set the day-to-day operational policy for
the Society, together with the other officers.[10]

Attendees at a third meeting selected officers, led by Bushrod Washington as president. Thirteen vice-presidents included Secretary of the
Treasury William Crawford and Speaker of the House Henry Clay. The
other vice-presidents included William Phillips of Massachusetts, Colo-
nel Henry Rutgers of New York, John Eager Howard, Samuel Smith, and
John C. Herbert of Maryland, John Taylor of Caroline, General John Mason of the District of Columbia, Andrew Jackson of Tennessee, Robert
Ralston and Richard Rush of Pennsylvania, and Robert Finley of New
Jersey.[11] By selecting such eminent politicians and others of national
reputation, the Society sought to gain prestige and appeal to public curi-
osity. This slate of prestigious officers lent the Society the aura of national leadership.[12] The actual work was, of course, carried out by the
board and the executive secretary. Several members of the board were
government employees. Elias Caldwell was Clerk of the Supreme Court;
William Thorton was Superintendent of the Patent Office; James Laurie
was a clerk in the Treasury department; and Obadiah Brown was a clerk
in the Post Office Department. Three board members were clergymen.
Elias Caldwell was elected secretary. All of these persons lived within
the District of Columbia, thus making it possible for them to be active in
the affairs of the Society.[13]

By proclaiming its goal as elevating and securing the personal rights
of free blacks, the Society sought to gain national support by portraying
itself as a humane institution. A few years later most free blacks and abolitionists insisted that colonization's propaganda describing blacks as
inferior and licentious only increased racial prejudice and hatred. Instead
of elevating free blacks, the Society was viewed as lowering the status of
free blacks.[14] Although this humanitarian effort appealed to northern sen-
sibilities, many of the Society's most important early advocates were
southerners with more pragmatic concerns about free blacks in a slave
society. Supporters from Maryland and Virginia contributed anywhere
from $200 to $500 to the Society, and this sort of southern support in the
early years reflected the almost universal fear among slaveholders that
free blacks posed a constant threat by helping fugitive slaves and provoking slave revolts.[15] Insurrections like the successful slave revolt in French
Santo Domingo during the 1790s and the failed Gabriel uprising near
Richmond in 1800 only heightened slave owners' fears. By colonizing

free blacks, southerners hoped to lessen this danger, and abolitionists later accused colonizationists of creating the Society merely to protect them from the fear that free blacks might seek slavery's destruction through insurrection.[16]

After electing officers and writing a constitution, the Colonization Society forwarded a memorial to Congress. Signed by Bushrod Washington and read before the House of Representatives by John Randolph, the document requested that the national government use public funds to remove free blacks to Africa through a program of systematic colonization. In this way blacks denied basic civil rights in the United States could find opportunities elsewhere. The memorial offered specifics for organizing and carrying out this purpose, leaving details of this grandiose plan to the "wisdom of the Congress." [17]

A month later the House's special Committee on the Slave Trade which received the memorial, recommended against establishing a new colony on the western coast of Africa. As an alternative the committee urged authorizing the president to negotiate with Great Britain for permission to resettle American free blacks in Sierra Leone. By transporting blacks to Sierra Leone, the cost and the difficulty of establishing a colony would be avoided. Should such a proposal be rejected, the committee alternately suggested that the United States seek an understanding with Britain and other maritime powers guaranteeing permanent neutrality for a new black colony on the western coast of Africa.[18]

Since Congress seemed unwilling at this time to commit the government to any course of action, the Colonization Society focused on building local auxiliaries throughout the country, both to raise funds and build public support for colonization. The Society patterned this effort after the national system of agencies pioneered by the American Bible Society. The Colonization Society appointed fifteen full time agents for its tasks. Such agents included Charles F. Mercer and William H. Fitzhugh of Virginia, Theodore Frelinguysen of New Jersey, Leonard Bacon of Connecticut, and Francis Scott Key of Washington, D.C. to name a few. These agencies became one of the most important sources of revenue for the Society.[19] Typical of these, William Meade, a Virginia Episcopal clergyman, founded local auxiliary societies throughout Virginia and Maryland, and then later in Georgia, and North and South Carolina. His efforts produced support societies in locales such as Augusta, Savannah, Fayetteville, Raleigh, and Chapel Hill. Meade worked to persuade the larger landowners and professional leaders in each community to lend their names and personal support in organizing local auxiliary societies and sought a prominent person in each community to serve as chairman.[20]

Meade followed up his successes in the South with further visits to the northeastern section of the country during November of 1819 where he established auxiliary societies in Boston, New Haven, Hartford, Providence, and Newburyport.[21] These societies, including auxiliaries in Philadelphia, New York, and Baltimore, found support among merchants, shippers, and bankers who were as interested in the advantages of commercial trade with Africa as in benefiting free blacks.

Arthur Tappan, a successful New York merchant, early and ardently supported colonization and once a colony was established in Africa, sought guarantees for his shipping firm from Ralph Gurley, secretary for the Colonization Society. Another strong friend and advocate of African colonization was John H. B. Latrobe, a Baltimore shipper. Auxiliaries in Philadelphia, New York, and Baltimore financially supported a fact-finding mission of Samuel Mills and Ebenezer Burgess to western Africa in 1817, while Isaac McKim, a prosperous Baltimore shipper, also lent money for the trip. Throughout much of its history, the Society would receive some of its strongest support from sources among the merchant and shipping interests of the eastern seaboard.

Other regions, as well, enthusiastically endorsed the Society's efforts as its ideas of African colonization spread into every region of the United States. Ultimately, sixteen state societies and more than two hundred local auxiliaries would be established. Auxiliary bodies were established in many western states such as Pennsylvania, Ohio, and Kentucky. Ohio counted auxiliaries in Cleveland, Canfield, Canton, Columbus, Bellrock, Lancaster, Full Creek, Germantown, Eaton, Bainbridge, and Oxford, and prominent Ohio politicians expediently enlisted. The personal zeal of Benjamin Peers, commissioned by the Colonization Society to advertise and build new auxiliaries, together with the Ohioans' fear of the growing population of free blacks in their state prompted the Society's success. Peers was paid twenty-five dollars a month along with expenses which were taken from the contributions he collected.[22] In cities like Cincinnati, the black slum community, called Little Africa, expanded rapidly as it drew blacks from Virginia and Maryland.

Yet this early success proved ephemeral. Soon many of these auxiliaries, particularly those in the South, fell into decline. Swift changes in response to the Industrial Revolution altered the national perspective on the institution of slavery. The Industrial Revolution, especially in Great Britain after 1785, produced phenomenal growth in the production of cotton cloth. British and other Europeans textile industries now required so much cotton that the West Indies, Brazil, and India could not meet the demand, and this insatiable new appetite for cotton would affect the United States profoundly.

Formerly only the long stable or "sea land" cotton could be culti-vated profitably because of the labor-intensive processes involved in ex-tracting seed from the fiber, and this sort of cotton grew well only in ar-eas near the sea. But with the advent of Eli Whitney's cotton gin, "up-land" cotton became a cash crop since the machine effectively removed the seeds regardless of the fiber's length. This short staple cotton grew bountifully in lands beyond the South's coastal regions, ultimately blan-keting most of the slave states. The response to world demands so drasti-cally altered the nation's economic growth that by 1840 the South was producing over sixty percent of the world's cotton.[23] As slave-produced cotton became so extraordinarily profitable, Dixie strengthened its com-mitment to its system of forced labor, lost interest in manumission, and shaped an iron resolve against any weakening of its system of human bondage. The Missouri debates on the slavery question in 1819 did noth-ing to alleviate the apprehensions of southern slaveholding interests, but rather, put them on the offensive. Slavery advocates now denounced Af-rican colonization as merely a stalking horse for abolition and withdrew all support. Hopes of gradual emancipation quickly vanished in the Deep South.

In addition, after William Mead, who had originally acted as travel-ing agent for the American Colonization Society, returned to his church duties, the organization maintained no paid full-time traveling represen-tative to nourish the new auxiliaries in the South, likely a hopeless task in light of cotton's new prosperity. Consequently, a number of southern auxiliaries, including those in Savanna and Augusta, ceased to exist.

In contrast, a number of northern state legislatures, along with the upper south state of Maryland, adopted resolutions in support of the colonization plan in January, 1818. Maryland, with a large free black population, a substantial number of merchants and shippers interested in commercial trade to West Africa, and no appreciable cotton production, requested the governor to write the president and Congress, urging nego-tiations for a tract of land for colonization on Africa's western coast.[24]

That same month the Ohio legislature instructed its senators and congressmen to seek federal support for African colonization. In 1824 the Ohio legislature once again adopted several resolutions in support of colonizing free blacks. The first requested Congress and other state legis-

latures to consider plans for gradual emancipation in their respective
states. The second proposed that the national government enact legislation under which all slaves would be set free at the age of twenty-one
years, although how the national government might implement such an
action, the legislature did not stipulate. The third resolution suggested
that since slavery was a national evil, the nation as a whole should share
the cost of its removal. Colonizationists persuaded legislatures of Pennsylvania, Vermont, New Jersey, Delaware, Illinois, Indiana, Connecticut,
and Massachusetts to endorse Ohio's resolutions.[25]

The well-organized colonizationists had substantial enough influence
with lawmakers to coordinate effective lobbying. These efforts also illus-
trate the growing popularity of colonization schemes in the 1820s. A
widespread concern was developing over the effects of the institution of
slavery and the conditions of free blacks as well. African colonization
seemed a moderate and viable solution to both these growing concerns.

Many church organizations also threw their support to the aims and
efforts of the colonization movement. Prestigious religious bodies, such
as the General Assembly of the Presbyterian Church, the General Synod
of the Reformed Dutch Church, and the Episcopal Convention of Virginia announced support for African colonization. Each of these organizations adopted resolutions endorsing the Colonization Society.[26] The
Massachusetts and Connecticut Conventions of Congregational Clergy
and the Ohio Methodist District Conference also approved the colonization plan. Although appropriating no funds, the conventions did publicly
endorse African colonization.

Some groups, however, authorized that special contributions be collected from church members on or near the Fourth of July for the support
of the Society. Such religionists ostensibly associated colonization with
patriotism.[27] The Lutheran Synod endorsed the Colonization Society, and
the Methodist Conference of 1834 at New Haven, Connecticut also recommended colonization to their members, insisting that abolitionists'
opposition to colonization would only injure the case of free blacks.[28]
The Conference further ordained that each preacher should collect an
offering on or near the Fourth of July for the benefit of the Colonization
Society.[29]

Clearly African colonization garnered impressive support among
leading Protestants. Evidently this support resulted not from compassion
toward blacks, but from the common belief that free blacks blighted society and degraded its morals. By transporting blacks to Africa, not only
would the white American society be preserved, but the blessings of

Christianity and civilization would be sent to "darkest" Africa. Fires of the second Great Awakening had also stimulated concern among conscientious people who shared the beliefs that equality for blacks would never be achieved in America. Through these annual Fourth of July collections from churches across the United States, the Society gained additional financial and public support, as their agents often spoke from these pulpits.

Other organizations also involved themselves with the colonization movement by providing financial and public support. Some Masonic lodges from Maryland, Virginia, Pennsylvania, Maine, Massachusetts, Mississippi, and Vermont made contributions for colonizing free blacks. Another source of support came from various female organizations. Women in Delaware, Virginia, and Maryland formed small auxiliaries to send money to the national Society in Washington. The Fredericksburg and the Falmouth female auxiliaries sent $500 to the Society. In Baltimore the women's auxiliary earned $2,500 by sewing and knitting articles at a fair.[30] So apart from its systems of national and auxiliary agencies, the Colonization Society enjoyed other sources of income through collections taken from various Protestant churches on the Fourth of July of each year, as well as through private donations, legacies, and state appropriations.[31]

Throughout the 1820s, the Society received wide support from the general public. Wealthy and prestigious men, leading politicians, church organizations, and women's auxiliaries supported the colonization movement. Those who endorsed the colonizing of free blacks were normally people with greater income and education. Such representatives of the prosperous middle class tended to be paternalistic in their social attitudes, believing that their status conferred a special obligation upon them to work toward creating a better society; that is, one with no black participants.

African colonization also had the concurrence and aid of numerous men of note. William H. Fitzhugh, an influential slave owner, argued that African colonization merited federal aid and could be justified constitutionally as promoting the republic's "common defense and general welfare." Fitzhugh estimated the slave population's increase at about 40,000 annually. The slave population would, instead, therefore decline, he argued, if 50,000 free blacks could be transported each year. Slave owners such as himself, he suggested, would be more willing to emancipate their slaves gradually, provided these freed slaves were transported to Africa where they posed no threat to slaveholders in the South. The cost of transporting these immigrants, about $100,000 annually, should be assumed by the national government. If regions like Louisiana and Florida could be acquired for the good of the country, so he insisted could territory in Africa. The money could be appropriated by the national government as it had done for roads and canals.[32] Fitzhugh's proposal came, it must be noted, before the spectacular success of upland cotton fattened the purses of the slaveocracy even as it undermined the possibility of emancipation.

Former President Madison lent the prestige of his name to the colonization cause. Slavery was a "sad blot on our free country," Madison lamented. Beyond this self-concern he also hoped to negate the reproaches that other nations heaped upon the United States as one of the few western nations to have a legal system of slavery. Like Jefferson, Madison saw colonization as an answer to ending slavery. Once a mechanism was set up to transport free blacks outside the United States, then slave owners would be more willing to free their slaves, thus ending slavery. During the War of Independence, the Virginia House of Delegates debated the plan for gradual emancipation which included a colonization plan. Madison endorsed the plan in 1789. Consequently Madison welcomed the formation of the American Colonization Society in 1816, as a vehicle for gradually freeing the country of slavery as well as being worthy of "encouragement from all who regarded slavery as an evil, who wished to see it diminish and abolished by peaceable and just means, and who have themselves no better mode to propose." Colonization was the way for a slave-free America. In his will, Madison left $2,000 to the Society. The money came from the proceeds of the publication of his *Debates in the Federal Convention*.[33] Together with Jefferson, Madison continued to hope that slavery would ultimately die out, but such hopes swiftly faded when English textile mills, running full swing, demanded more slave produced cotton.

Yet the hope for a truly free nation died hard, and Madison continued to insist that slavery could and must end. A fundamental obstacle blocked gradual emancipation: where would the slaves go after emancipation and who would pay the costs for transporting them. The answer, at least to Madison, was to colonize them on the western coast of Africa.[34] Madison urged Congress to advance an amendment granting itself the authority to fund colonization through the sale of public lands. His fellow Virginian and long-time political adversary, Chief Justice John Marshall of the Supreme Court, shared this view. Late in their lives Madison and Marshall, both active in the colonization movement, proposed that funds from the sale of public lands be used to emancipate and deport freed blacks.[35] Marshall, president of the Richmond and Manchester auxiliary, made many donations to the colonization cause. Madison served as vice-president of the Richmond and Manchester auxiliary and from 1833 to 1836 as national president of the Society. Madison had consistently believed that colonization was the answer to making America black-free and slave-free.

To raise funds and increase public support for the Society's goals, Ralph Randolph Gurley, the newly appointed secretary, established the *African Repository and Colonial Journal* as the official organ of the Society in 1825. Gurley, son of a Connecticut Congregational minister, graduated from Yale and received his license to preach. But rather than preach, he joined the Colonization Society as traveling agent and lecturer for colonization in New England. Moving through the northeast, he met thousands of people, developed his skills as an orator, and raised money for colonization. He also worked closely with Caldwell, gaining valuable experience in the Society's operations so that when Caldwell died in 1825, Gurley was named secretary. Gurley devoted himself to its advancement, on one occasion even selling his furniture and books to help pay the Society's debt. For the next fifty years, Gurley would build his career around African colonization.

Through the new journal Gurley worked energetically to build colonization into a coherent national movement by effectively publicizing its purpose and progress. Printing letters of interest and of praise, extracts from African travel books, and reprints of newspaper articles supporting colonization, Gurley also listed the names of financial contributors and maintained an updated roster of newly formed auxiliaries. Gurley financed the journal through private subscriptions.[36]

While a vibrant journal might gain colonization a degree of public support, the key to success lay in political action, and after 1832 the political party most closely associated with the Colonization Society was the Whig party. African colonization was consistent with the Whig's broad program of social and political action since many Whigs believed in an active government to develop the country economically and socially. Social harmony was especially important to the Whigs since economic prosperity could only be built by a stable and uniform society. Free blacks, according to many Whigs, would never be accepted into white society on equal terms because of racial prejudices, so the only acceptable solution seemed to be emigration to Africa. There free blacks could form their own self-governing society and pursue their distinctive

economic opportunities. Removal would benefit free blacks, while ensur-
ing a more stable and homogeneous society in the United States, according to the idea's proponents.

Colonization counted important Whigs in its camp, among them
Daniel Webster, Edward Everett, and the "Old Henry Clay Whig," Abraham Lincoln.[37] But the foremost Whig Colonization Society advocate
was Henry Clay, the living embodiment of the Whig cause. Clay became,
in many ways, the Society's greatest asset and was its most popular
speaker at its anniversaries.[38] He had served as acting chairman when the
Society was formed and became president of the Society from 1836 to
1852, succeeding James Madison. Because of Clay's Whig ideology of
using government to shape a better society, he favored federal aid to
support African colonization. He inserted a provision in his Distribution
Bill of 1832, dividing the proceeds from the sale of public lands among
the states to be earmarked for internal improvements, education, or colonization. The bill passed Congress but did not survive President Jackson's veto. Jackson viewed the bill as both impractical and unconstitutional. African colonization never came closer to fruition than this failed
legislation.[39] Since the African colonization program was so closely tied
to Clay in the public mind, it might well have taken on new life had he
been elected president.

Clay, of course, never attained the presidency, but the Society he
championed went through several different phases of development over
the years. In its formation period during the 1820s, the Society gained
strength and popularity in both northern and southern sections of the
country. According to information provided by the Colonization Society,
the amount of money collected from 1820 to 1830 was $112,842.89. The
expenditures which amounted to $106,367.72 included salaries for the
Society officers (the secretary and the traveling agents), the cost of transportation, buildings, roads, schools, and other supplies. Some 1,430 emigrants had been transported at an estimated cost of $74.38 a person.[40]
Northern philanthropic groups supported colonization as an effective
way to elevate free blacks who migrated to northern states. Because of
widespread prejudice and lack of economic opportunity, free blacks collected in larger towns and cities, becoming tenants in slum sections. This
created yet further difficulties as many northern whites then associated
crime and poverty with the free black population. Magazine articles were
reprinted in the *African Repository*, giving statistics of the proportion of
the free blacks in prisons. For example a reprint showed the population
of Pennsylvania to be about 800,000 with the number of free blacks

about 26,000; yet free blacks made up about half of the convict population in the state prison. Through articles like this, Gurley sought to show the need for colonizing free blacks.[41] At the same time southern whites came to support the transporting of free blacks out of the country in order to lessen the perceived threat of slave insurrections encouraged by the presence and activity of free blacks.

Between 1830 and 1840 serious financial difficulties hindered the Society's progress. By 1834 the Society had accumulated $45,645.75 in debt. The Society had overextended itself in chartering ships, buying supplies, transporting emigrants, and overestimating the amounts they expected to collect in contributions.[42] The Society's struggle throughout the 1830s and 1840s to remain solvent diverted much of its energy from its fundamental tasks.

Internal divisions among the ranks of colonizationists themselves also produced additional financial problems. Militant abolitionists such as William Lloyd Garrison dismissed colonization as a spineless compromise with slavery, and many prominent colonizationists including Arthur and Lewis Tappan, James G. Birney, and Gerrit Smith renounced and abandoned the cause, taking their money with them to the abolitionist camp. The Society received the lowest level of contributions since its inception, merely $10,947.41, in 1838.[43] While abolitionist dissertations contributed to this, the Panic of 1837 no doubt impacted this short fall also as Americans tightened their pocket books under financial stress.

Adding to the defections was the secession of a number of state auxiliaries from the national Society. Fears of northern abolitionist influence within the Colonization Society resulted in the departure of auxiliary societies in the South. Severing ties with the national body, the Auxiliary Colonization Society of Richmond and Manchester assumed control of its own policy and changed its name to the Colonization Society of the State of Virginia in 1828. Vice-presidents included James Madison, James Monroe, and John Tyler.[44] Mississippi and Louisiana soon followed Virginia in her secession from the national organization by similar actions.[45]

James Madison's decision to accept the national presidency of the American Colonization Society in 1833, even while actively supporting the now separate Colonization Society of Virginia and seeking state appropriations for colonization, illustrates the South's growing ambivalence concerning slavery. Reflecting the ideals of the revolutionary generation and its Enlightenment roots, Madison looked to colonization as a long term but feasible way of ridding the country of slavery. During the

1830s, however, other southerners began to advocate slavery as a positive good as its profitability soared.

Thomas Roderick Dew, professor of political law at William and
Mary College, reflected this view in a pamphlet he wrote and sent to
Madison. Defending slavery as morally and economically sound, Dew
also attacked colonization as a "stupendous piece of folly." A month after receiving the pamphlet, Madison accepted the presidency of the national Society and responded to Dew by defending colonization as a viable means of gradually ending slavery. Madison's name and prestige
gave the national colonization program renewed credibility as a viable
solution to slavery's many-faceted problems.[46]

In the mind of whites, one of slavery's most traumatic effects was
black rebellion. The Maryland legislature, reacting to Nat Turner's 1832
uprising, appropriated $20,000 a year for ten years, to be allocated for
colonizing Maryland's emancipated slaves. After 1833 the Maryland
State Society acted independently of the national Society by hiring its
own agents to gather funds for an African venture. The state eventually
established its own colony, Maryland in Liberia, in western Africa.
Unlike other southern states, Maryland chose this autonomous path as a
means of pursuing a more aggressive colonization policy which would
embrace gradual emancipation. The national Society, however, fearful of
losing its southern support, refused to broaden its goal.[47]

Apart from southern auxiliary secessions, some northern entities
opted for independence from the mother organization. The Colonization
Society allowed its colony in Africa to trade in alcohol, but many northern colonizationists also strongly supported the temperance movement.[48]
So Pennsylvanians formed the Young Men's Colonization Society of in
1833, independent of the national Society. The Pennsylvania Society
prohibited trade in alcohol and arms, both which were carried on by the
parent Society in Washington. In the same year the New York Colonization Society severed its ties with the parent Society for similar reasons.
The Young Men's Colonization Society of Boston became independent,
pursuing a stronger antislavery course than did the national Society.[49]
Through such defections the Colonization Society lost much of its political and social prestige by the end of the 1840s, and it lost much of the
public's attention.[50]

Interest in the Colonization Society revived during the 1850s as
quarrels over slavery intensified and popular opinion increasingly polarized. Several state legislatures began to re-examine the potentials of
colonization. In 1850 Virginia's legislature appropriated $30,000 annu-

ally for the next five years for the deportation of free blacks to Africa. In 1852 the New Jersey's legislature appropriated $1,000 annually for two years to transport free blacks to Africa, increasing this sum to $4,000 in 1855. Both Pennsylvania and Missouri appropriated smaller amounts for the same purpose. Maryland's legislature in 1852 appropriated $10,000 annually for six years to deport free blacks to Africa, as interest in colonization revived with the increase of tension between slave and free states.[51]

Prominent political leaders such as Daniel Webster, Edward Everett, Stephen A. Douglas, James M. Wayne, and Millard Fillmore once again appeared at the Society's annual meetings. In a speech at a gathering on February 27, 1852, Webster called for federal appropriations from the sale of public lands to support African colonization. "I know of no reason why this enterprise," he remarked, "should not receive the fostering care of the Government."[52] President Fillmore prepared a proposal recommending federal appropriations for colonization in his 1852 State of the Union Address. Congress then could encourage emancipation in the South by offering to remove freed slaves. Should 100,000 freed slaves be transported yearly, "that would not only prevent the increase of the slave population," Fillmore maintained, "but constantly diminish it, and at last . . . wipe it out entirely." He and his cabinet decided, however, to excise this proposal from his message because of heightened tensions fostered by the slavery issue.[53]

Speaking at Peoria, Illinois in 1854, Abraham Lincoln asserted the difficulty of eradicating the institution of slavery in any satisfactory way. "My first impulse," Lincoln declared, "would be to free all the slaves, and send them to Liberia—to their own native land." Yet upon further reflection, he decided, the plan seemed impractical because of the tremendous cost involved.[54] Three years later Lincoln, speaking at Springfield, Illinois, maintained that if there was to be a separation between the white and black races it "must be effected by colonization." It would be a difficult task, he argued, "but 'when there is a will there is a way'; and what colonization needs most is a hearty will."[55] Lincoln personally favored colonization, believing it "morally right"; but he also saw it as impractical because of the great cost in removing blacks in large numbers to Africa.

Reflecting this magnified national concern, the Society's contributions increased from $29,000 in 1847 to $97,000 in 1851, and reached the highest annual level of $160,000 in 1859. The slavery question and the intensity associated with it temporarily stimulated revived interest in

African colonization as a moderate alternative between slavery and immediate abolition. Lincoln no doubt articulated the feelings of a majority of his fellow white Americans by proclaiming in the Lincoln-Douglas debates: "I am not, nor ever have been in favor of bringing about in any way the social and political equality of the white and black races." He postulated "a physical difference between the white and black races" which would "forever forbid the two races living together on terms of social and political equality."[56]

As much as many northerners disliked the institution of slavery, they equally disdained immediate abolition with its assumptions of both freedom and equal rights for blacks. Their goal was less the eradication of human bondage and more the securing of an America as a black-free continent. At the same time, supporters of colonization felt a benevolent responsibility toward the descendents of kidnapped Africans. In the process of purging American society, the leaders of white society believed that they had a moral obligation to grant to black expatriates the gift of a democratic republic, so long as that beneficence stood segregated from them by the Atlantic Ocean.

NOTES

1. Staudenraus, *African Colonization*, 24-25.

2. "Notice," *Daily National Intelligencer*, 4 (December 18, 1816): 3.

3. Speech at Organization of American Colonization Society, December 21, 1816, *The Papers of Henry Clay*, James F. Hopkins, ed., (Lexington: University of Kentucky Press, 1961), 2:263-264.

4. Alexander, *History of Colonization*, 80-82; Speech at Organization of American Colonization Society, December 21, 1816, *Papers of Henry Clay*, 2:263-264.

5. Drew R. McCoy, *The Last of the Fathers: James Madison and the Republican Legacy* (Cambridge: Cambridge University Press, 1989), 284; Litwack, *North of Slavery*, 21-23.

6. Alexander, *History of Colonization*, 86.

7. These, however, did not last very long for reasons that will be explained later in this chapter.

8. Robert Dawidoff, *The Education of John Randolph* (New York: W. W. Norton, 1979), 50-51; "Transplanting Free Negroes to Ohio From 1815 to 1858," *Journal of Negro History* 1 (July 1916): 308-309; Glyndon G. Van Deusen , *The Life of Henry Clay* (Boston: Little Brown and Company, 1937), 137; Clement Eaton, *Henry Clay and the Art of American Politics* (Boston: Little Brown and Company, 1957), 136; Carl Schurz, *Henry Clay* (New York: Frederich Ungar Publishing Co., reprinted, 1968), 1:302-305.

9. David M. Striefford, "The American Colonization Society: An Application of Republican Ideology of Early Antebellum Reform," *Journal of Southern History* 45 (May 1979): 201-203.

10. Alexander, *History of Colonization*, 89-90.

11. Staudenraus, *African Colonization*, 29-30.

12. Bancroft, "Early Antislavery Movement," 163-164; Sweet, *Black Images*, 37.

13. Staudenraus, *African Colonization*, 30.

14. Litwack, *North of Slavery*, 24-27.

15. Bancroft, "Early Antislavery Movement," 157-166.

16. Gerald Sorin, *Abolitionism: A New Perspective* (New York: Praeger Publishers, 1972), 40-41; Delindus R. Brown, "Free Black's Rhetorical Impact on African Colonization: The Emergence of Rhetorical Exigence." *Journal of Black Studies* 9 (March 1979): 251-263.

17. Memorial of the American Society for Colonizing the Free People of Color, January 1817, in J. K. Gales (comp.), *Debates and Proceedings of the Congress of the United States, 1789-1824: Annals of the Congress of the United States* (42 vols., Washington: Gales and Seaton, 1834-56), 30 (14 Cong., 2 Sess.): 481-3; Cited hereafter as *Annals of Congress*; "Memorial of the President and Board of Managers of the American Society for Colonizing the Free People

of Color of the Unites States," *Daily National Intelligencer*, 5 (January 18, 1817): 2; Alexander, *History of Colonization*, 94.

18. Staudenraus, *African Colonization*, 34.

19. Early Lee Fox, *The American Colonization Society, 1817-1840* (Baltimore: The John Hopkins Press, 1919), 57-60.

20. Staudenraus, *African Colonization*, 70-72.

21. *Ibid.*, 72-73.

22. *Ibid.*, 136-149.

23. Constance Mc L. Green, *Eli Whitney and the Birth of American Technology* (Glenview: Little/Brown, 1956), 12-18.

24. "Resolution passed unanimously by the legislature of Maryland," *African Repository* 1 (October 1825): 250.

25. Herman V. Ames, *State Documents on Federal Relations: The States and the United States* (New York: Da Capo Press, 1970), 203-204; *African Repository* 1 (October 1825): 251.

26. "Public Sentiment," *African Repository* 1 (June 1825): 125.

27. "Massachusetts Conventions," "Connecticut Convention," "Ohio Methodists Convention," *African Repository* 3 (June, 1827): 118-120.

28. "Resolution of the Lutheran Synod," *African Repository* 3 (October, 1827): 252.

29. "New York Conference," *African Repository* 10 (June, 1834): 127.

30. Staudenraus, *African Colonization*, 111-113.

31. Fox, *American Colonization Society*, 57.

32. William Fitzhugh, "The Colonization Scheme," *African Repository* 2 (October 1826): 254-256.

33. James McCoy, *The Last of the Fathers: James Madison and the Republican Legacy* (Cambridge: Cambridge University Press, 1989), 279-282; Irving Brant, *James Madison: Commander in Chief, 1812-1836* (Indianapolis: The Bobbs-Merrill Company, Inc., 1961), 514; Mellon, *Views on Negro Slavery*, 133-136.

34. McCoy, *The Last of the Fathers*, 5-6, 299; Staudenraus, *African Colonization*, 106-107, 183; Mellon, *Views on Negro Slavery*, 126.

35. "Letters From Ex-President Madison and Chief Justice Marshall," *African Repository* 12 (March, 1836): 90-91; Brant, *James Madison*, 431; McCoy, *The Last of the Fathers*, 280.

36. Staudenraus, *African Colonization*, 76-78, 97-101, 103.

37. Daniel Walker Howe, *The Political Culture of the American Whigs* (Chicago: The University of Chicago Press, 1979), 136-137.

38. Bancroft, "Early Antislavery Movement," 185.

39. Thomas D. Matijastic, "Whig Support for African Colonization: Ohio As a Test Case," *Mid-America: A Historical Review* 66 (April-July, 1984): 82; Staudenraus, *African Colonization*, 185-187.

40. Fox, *Colonization Society*, 88-89.

41. "From the New York Tract Magazine," *African Repository* 1 (May, 1825): 91-92.

42. "The Seventeenth Annual Meeting of the Colonization Society." *African Repository* 10 (February, 1834): 8-17.

43. Staudenraus, *African Colonization*, 251.

44. "Colonization Society of Virginia," *African Repository* 4 (December, 1828): 307.

45. Staudenraus, *African Colonization*, 236; Fox, *American Colonization*, 95.

46. James Madison to Thomas R. Dew, February 23, 1833, in *Writings of Madison*, Gaillard Hunt, ed. (New York: G. P. Putnam's, 1900-1910), 9: 498-502; McCoy, *The Last of the Fathers*, 299-301; Brant, *James Madison*, 509-510.

47. "Maryland Colonization Society," *African Repository* 17 (November, 1833): 184-189; Staudenraus, *African Colonization*, 232-233; Alexander, *History of Colonization*, 405-407; Fox, *American Colonization*, 96.

48. Staudenraus, *African Colonization*, 234-237; Alexander, *History of Colonization*, 445-454.

49. Staudenraus, *African Colonization*, 204-205.

50. Bancroft, "Early Antislavery Movement," 184.

51. Staudenraus, *African Colonization*, 244.

52. Daniel Webster, *The Writings and Speeches of Daniel Webster*, 18 Vols. (Boston: Little, Brown, and Company, 1903), 13: 505-506.

53. Robert J. Rayback, *Millard Fillmore: Biography of a President* (Buffalo: Henry Steward, 1959), 367-370.

54. "Speech at Peoria," October 16, 1854, *The Collected Works Abraham Lincoln*, Roy P. Basler, ed. (4 vols., New Brunswick: Rutgers University Press, 1953), 2: 255.

55. "Speech at Springfield, Illinois, June 26, 1857, *ibid.*, 409.

56. "Fourth Debate with Stephen A. Douglas" Charleston, Illinois, September 18, 1858, *ibid.*, 3: 145-146.

Chapter 3
Back to Africa

In spite of the United States government's reluctance to sponsor an independent refuge for former slaves in Africa, by 1825 a black America had taken root on the western coast of the "Dark Continent" through the efforts of the American Colonization Society.[1] After Congress rejected the first memorial in January, 1817 requesting aid for African colonization, the Colonization Society decided to launch a pilot colony program to demonstrate the concept's feasibility. The Society would dispatch a fact-finding mission to the western coast of Africa to collect the information necessary for selecting colonization territory. The region which interested the Society would have to be conducive to agriculture so that the colony could be maintained through agrarian production. Funded partially by the Society, Samuel J. Mills, fund raiser for missionary and other New England benevolent societies, and Spanish-speaking Ebenezer Burgess, professor at Burlington College, volunteered to sail to Britain and Africa on a fact-finding venture before the next session of Congress.[2] The Society did not have the $5,000 needed to pay the trip's full cost, so assisted by Francis Scott Key, Mills established auxiliaries in Baltimore, Philadelphia, and New York, the nation's three richest commercial centers. Their efforts fell short, and the Society was forced to borrow $2,500 from Isaac McKim, a Baltimore shipper who would be interested in future trade with Africa and would later become one of the Society's vice-presidents.[3]

After spending a month in Great Britain collecting information about sites near Sierra Leone, Mills and Burgess sailed on to Africa. They arrived at Freetown, the principal settlement in Sierra Leone, the British colony for free blacks founded earlier in the century under the guidance of Granville Sharp and William Wilberforce. The African colonists there appeared to be well-fed and educated, and Mills and Burgess found schools and churches providing Africans with "instruction in reading, writing, and arithmetic," both in Freetown and its surrounding villages.[4] The two investigators were encouraged about a possible American African colonization project.

The Americans then hired a small schooner and, with the help of John Kizell, spent six weeks studying the coastal region near Sierra Leone. Kizell, a former slave from South Carolina and now a merchant in Sierra Leone, was well acquainted with the surrounding territory. They stopped at several villages, talked with local chiefs in the area, and collected specimens of rice, cotton, and sugar cane to take back with them to America to show the potential for lucrative farming in this locale.

Mills and Burgess also visited Sherbro Island, about twenty-two miles in length and twelve miles in width, not far from Sierra Leone. Kizell, a native of the island taken from there as a slave to South Carolina, recommended it as a possible colonization site. He assured Mills and Burgess that he could secure a place for a colony on the island. Kizell, however, proved unable to persuade the local chiefs to part with any of their land. Even so, on their return to the United States, Mills and Burgess urged establishing a colony at Sherbro Island.

Burgess returned with a glowing report about the western coast of Africa, but Mills had contracted fever while in Africa and died on the homeward voyage. Burgess described western Africa as a fertile land drained by large rivers and producing rice, sugar cane, fruits, spices, gold dust, and ivory. Burgess's plan seemed feasible since the slave trade was depopulating the coastal villages. He insisted that colonial settlements planted along the coast would halt the slave traffic, and this idea became a motivating force in the campaign against that trade.

On March 3, 1819 Congress passed the Slave Trade Act. Introduced by Charles Fenton Mercer, an active Virginian colonizationist, this legislation authorized the president to use the navy to return to Africa those rescued from the slave trade in American waters. Congress also appropriated $100,000 to carry out this program, but provided no details explaining what action the president should take.[5]

The Society sent Bushrod Washington, Francis Scott Key, John Mason, and Walter Jones, all eminent constitutional lawyers, to urge President Monroe to interpret the act as authorizing him to purchase land in Africa for the resettlement of rescued Africans. The recaptured slaves, they argued, could not simply be dumped on the African coast without a colonial structure providing for their resettlement. John Quincy Adams, Monroe's secretary of state, rejected this interpretation as unconstitutional, insisting the Constitution authorized no purchase of land for colonial purposes. While the United States had purchased Louisiana and the territory at the mouth of the Columbia River, these regions, Adams argued, were "contiguous to and continuous with our own." Such precedents, he insisted, did not "warrant the purchase of countries beyond the seas, or the establishment of a colonial system of government subordinate to and dependent upon that of the United States."[6] Adams convinced a majority of his cabinet colleagues, including Attorney General William Wirt, Secretary of War John C. Calhoun, and Secretary of the Navy Smith Thompson.

Monroe initially accepted this recommendation, but later the arguments of Adam's cabinet rival, Secretary of the Treasury William H. Crawford would induce him to reverse his decision. One of the Colonization Society's vice-presidents, Crawford endorsed a special appeal for reconsideration from Francis Scott Key. The two men persuaded both Monroe and Attorney General Wirt that provision for sufficient food and shelter "at or near the place where they landed" would be essential to aid recaptured slaves taken in suppressing the international traffic in returning them to their former homes. The nation was committed by treaty to cooperate with Great Britain for these purposes, and only on these grounds were the "benevolent" requirements of the Slave Trade Act constitutional. In a special message early in 1819, Monroe announced the sending of two agents and a team of workers to prepare the government's station for returning recaptured slaves to Africa. Monroe assured Congress that the agents would be authorized only "to select the most suitable place on the coast of Africa at which all persons who may be taken under this act shall be delivered to them, with an express injunction to exercise no power founded on the principle of colonization or other power than that of performing the benevolent offices above cited."[7]

Monroe's acceptance of this broad and liberal interpretation of the Slave Trade Act scarcely aligns with his veto, only three years later, of the Cumberland Road Bill appropriating money to repair and maintain a section of the national road. Acting with "deep regret, approving as I do the policy," Monroe insisted the Constitution granted no power for this purpose either "specifically" or "incidental to some power which has been specifically granted."[8] Apparently international affairs and domestic policy represented two distinct constitutional categories in Monroe's mind. Or it may be that the southern president's desire to return blacks to western Africa was simply stronger than his urge for road building.

Monroe appointed, on the Colonization Society's recommendation, Samuel Bacon, an Episcopal minister, and John P. Bankson, a government worker, as agents responsible for returning recaptured slaves to Africa. Authorized to hire free American blacks as laborers and carpenters to build an operating station in Africa, Bacon chartered the merchant ship *Elizabeth,* and the navy secretary ordered the USS *Cyane* along as escort. Bacon embarked with food and implements sufficient to support three hundred people for an entire year. After six months, however, only eighty-six recruits had been hired as laborers in an employment effort conducted largely through churches and antislavery groups. Of the eighty-six recruits, only twenty-eight were men; the rest were women and children, hired as seamstresses, nurses, and laundry workers. No plan was made for their return, and through this, the Society began the process of sending free blacks to Africa with the help of government funds.[9]

Eventually, three groups of settlers settled in Liberia. The first group consisted of free blacks (one third were mulattoes) who came from the larger cities of eastern United States. The second group was made up largely of emancipated slaves (emancipated on the condition they immigrated to Africa). The third group were African slaves returned to Africa. Despite Monroe's careful distinction, the majority of blacks transported to Africa through these funds were free blacks living in the United States.[10]

The *Elizabeth* set sail from New York for the western coast of Africa January 31, 1820. The Society sent physician Samuel Crozer on the mission with instructions to purchase land on Sherbro Island and to organize the colonists in their new settlement. Daniel Coker, a mulatto Methodist minister and teacher in the African School in Baltimore, also accompanied the immigrants. Thus an American black colony was tentatively rooted on the western coast of Africa by a private benevolent society in cooperation with the United States government under the guise of an asylum for recaptured Africans. Monroe, by using funds appropriated in the Slave Trade Act of 1819, empowered this effort and has been credited as one of colony's founding fathers.

After a six week crossing, the *Elizabeth* arrived at Sherbro Island, but as yet, neither the Society nor the American government owned any land in Africa. John Kizell, the interpreter for Mills and Burgess, soon purchased a small piece of land from the tribal chiefs at Campelar for the Society and hired tribesmen to clear the land and build a small village of mud huts. This locale proved a poor choice, lacking nearby potable water and sited in a low, marshy area which led to serious problems during the wet season, chiefly fever. In spite of this the colonists remained there until they could negotiate a better area.

In early March, at the rainy season's outset, the eighty-six colonists arrived at Campelar, but by September, forty-nine colonists, along with Bankson, Bacon, and Crozer had died from fever. African fever, as it came to be called, inflicted high fever and raging headaches and attacked almost all newcomers who were not adapted to this tropical climate. Even those who survived the fever were often debilitated for weeks. The colonists, as a result, fled to Sierra Leone, settling outside of Freetown.[11] This first American effort to establish a colony in Africa ended catastrophically.

In spite of the disaster, President Monroe, urged on by the Society, ordered a new expedition. The Society commissioned Ephraim Bacon, a minister and Samuel Bacon's brother, and Jonathan B. Winn, assisted by Christian Wiltberger and Joseph R. Andrus, to set up a post in Africa. On January 21, 1821, these agents along with thirty-three emigrants, mostly free blacks rather than recaptured slaves, sailed in the brig *Nautilus* for Africa. Lacking specific settlement plans, they intended to explore the area looking to buy territory for settlement. Upon arriving at Sierra Leone on March 9, 1821, they arranged to keep the emigrants at Fourah Bay until they selected a site for settlement. But the Sherbro Island chiefs refused to sell any additional land to the colonists, forcing the Society to abandon the island as a settlement site. Bacon and Andrus employed the schooner *Augusta* to explore the coast of southern Sierra Leone for a more suitable colonization site.

The Mangers of the Society then appointed Eli Ayres, a Baltimore physician, to go to Africa to attempt to negotiate for an appropriate site. As a naval surgeon, Ayres journeyed to Africa on a United States navy schooner. Arriving in Sierra Leone, he found Andrus and Winn dead from fever; Bacon, after contracting fever, had meanwhile sailed to the West Indies where he recovered and returned to the United States. The Society's board of managers persuaded Monroe's administration to send Lieutenant Robert Field Stockton, a naval officer, to Africa on the navy's new schooner, *Alligator*, with instructions to purchase territory for a settlement site.

Meeting at Sierra Leone, Stockton and Ayres moved on to Cape Mesurado, which the British recommended, to negotiate a land deal with the locals. The Portuguese had come to this region in the 15th century and given the coast some of its names, including Cape Mesurado. Other Europeans, including the English and the Dutch, came to the coast trad-

ing for gold, ivory, peppers, and slaves. The two main tribes around Cape
Mesurado were the Mamba and the Dey. By the 18th century the slave
trade was a rich business controlled by a native Africa confederacy
called the Condo Confederation with its headquarters at Bopulu in western Liberia. The slave trade was strongly established among the Man-
dingo tribesmen, but also included other tribes such as the Dey. The
slaves were predominately prisoners of war captured in inter-tribal war-
fare in the interior of Africa. Many Dyula traders were Muslims from the
hinterland. The Colonization Society hoped to end the slave trade by establishing a strong colony on the coast to resist the slave traffic and to
replace it with what it considered legitimate trade. King Peter, chief of
the Dey people at the Cape, was reluctant to cede any land, so after several days of delay, Stockton pulled out his two pistols and pointed one at
King Peter and the other at the people.[12] Under extortion, King Peter and
five other chiefs transferred Cape Mesurado to Stockton and Ayres. The
land was ceded not to the United States government or to the Colonization Society; rather, it was granted to Stockton and Ayres to hold for
colonization purposes.

Under these arrangements, the colony had no legal status. The
United States did not claim sovereignty over the colony, nor did other
nations recognize it as a sovereign entity. Although it was supplied by
the American government, Cape Mesurado was a private settlement under the control of the American Colonization Society.[13] The kings received goods worth less than three hundred dollars for the land and were
forced to pledge that they would live in peace with the new colony. The
kings were paid with six muskets, one box of beads, two hogshead of
tobacco, one cask of gunpowder, six iron bars, ten iron pots, one dozen
knives and forks, one dozen spoons, six pieces of blue baft, four hats,
three pairs of shoes, one box of pipes, one keg of nails, twenty looking
glasses, three handkerchiefs, three pieces of calico, three canes, four um-
brellas, one box of soup and one barrel of rum. Rum would become a
commodity in much demand.[14]

With the way now cleared, the settlers waiting in Sierra Leone sailed
on to Cape Mesurado. But the tribal peoples, fearing that having a colony
near by would hinder their slave trade quickly changed their minds about
selling the land to the settlers and forced the colonists to settle temporarily on an island near Cape Mesurado. After more bargaining and with
help from a powerful chieftain, the settlers eventually moved to Cape
Mesurado where they began clearing land and building huts. Food soon
ran short, and the locals again grew hostile to the new settlers. Ayres

urged the immigrants to return to Sierra Leone, but Elijah Johnson, one of the settlers, persuaded the others into staying and making Cape Mesurado their permanent home. Johnson unofficially took charge of the new colony after Ayres returned to Sierra Leone and then to the United States.[15]

In the meantime Jehudi Ashmun arrived at Cape Mesurado on August 9, 1822 on the *Strong*, along with recaptured Africans and released slaves. Ashmun, from Champlain, New York, had attended Middlebury College and Vermont University, then entered the Congregational ministry and became editor of a theological journal in Baltimore.[16] Ashmun came to Cape Mesurado with plans to establish a trading station for a Baltimore trading company.[17] He requested the Colonization Society to grant him a monopoly of all trade with the colony; he would pocket a third of the profits while the Society received the remaining two-thirds. Ashmun's plan for the new colony blended commercial advantages, humanitarian benevolence, and the spread of Christianity.

Ashmun, however, arrived at Cape Mesurado just as the colonists were expecting an attack from the local Africans resulting from a resurgence of hostility between the new settlement and neighboring tribes. He temporarily shelved his plans and spent the next few months building defensive fortifications for the colony, and on November 11, 1822 the natives attacked the settlement, hoping to drive the newcomers off the land. With a few old field cannons and forty muskets, thirty-five men were able to fight off two separate attacks until a British schooner, the *Prince Regent*, came to the aid of the colonists during the second attack. The ship's captain negotiated a truce between the African chiefs and the colonists, backed by the British at Sierra Leone, whom the natives feared. The accord ensured that the settlers would remain at Cape Mesurado, so Ashmun abandoning his trading venture, spent the next six years at Cape Mesurado helping establish the colony.[18]

Ayres returned from the United States on May 24, 1823 under appointment as agent for both the United States government and the Society. The colony then counted one hundred fifty houses, three storehouses for food and equipment, and a stone tower mounted with cannons. But Ayres again left Africa because of ill health and returned to the United States naming Ashmun as colony head.

Like Aryres, however, the colony also had fallen on difficult times. The Society lacked the money to send further supplies, leading to depleted food stores, and Ashmun's decision to ration food angered the settlers. Their unhappiness deepened when newcomers received equal distribution with the original settlers in land surveys and assignments. Finally, dissatisfaction exploded into mutiny when twelve armed settlers seized the food storehouses.

Ashmun quickly fell under heavy criticism from the Colonization Society's Board of Managers back in the United States. Settlers had sent letters charging him with oppression and theft of the goods forwarded by the Society. As a result, the Society dispatched its secretary, Ralph Randolph Gurley, to Africa to investigate these charges and to examine the colony's condition. In the meantime the mutineers had forced Ashmun from the colony, and he met Gurley at Porto Praya, Cape Verde Islands, on July 24, 1824. The two then sailed on to Cape Mesurado.

Gurley's investigations unearthed no evidence of impropriety or mismanagement on Ashmun's part. In order to stabilize the situation, he and Ashmun wrote a new constitution for the colony. Gurley then pardoned the participants in the mutiny and appointed Ashmun as agent. The Board of Managers initially rejected Gurley's actions because of their lingering distrust of Ashmun. But as reports came in of the restoration of order in the colony, the managers approved Gurley's reforms, cleared Ashmun of all charges, and approved his designation as their colonial agent. These changes brought renewed vigor, and it appeared that the colony had turned a critical point in its development.[19]

The colony now boasted a stone pier, two new church buildings, and several schools. It had also developed a flourishing trade with the tribes in the vicinity and was attracting new emigrants who were given lands to clear and farm. The Society provided tools to clear the land and build houses, and Ashmun encouraged colonists in farming endeavors. The Board of Managers envisioned the colony as a large tropical plantation much like the West Indies with an economy based on crops such as coffee, sugar, and cotton. The colonists, however, preferred commerce and trading, bringing in barrels of rum, tobacco, and cotton cloth to exchange with neighboring tribes for ivory, camwood, palm oil, and rice. In February, 1824 the Society named the colony Liberia after the Latin *liber,* or freeman. The chief settlement they named Monrovia in honor of President James Monroe. General Robert Goodloe Harper, a prominent Baltimore lawyer and the son-in-law of Charles Carroll of Carrollton, proposed both names. Harper, an active supporter and fund raiser for the Society, had worked to make Maryland a stronghold for African colonization.[20]

The African venture expanded in both numbers and territory in 1825 as the Society sent sixty-six emigrants to Cape Mesurado, and in order to provide them with farms, Ashmun purchased land from chiefs who owned acreage around St. Paul's River. In May of the same year, Ashmun bought from King Peter a large area above Monrovia called Cape Mount. Through war with the little Bassa tribesmen, Ashmun seized the Young Sesters territory below Monrovia, and in 1826 he established a trading post at the intersection of the Junk and St. Paul's rivers.[21]

The colony at Mesurado had grown from about two square miles in 1822 to 150 square miles by the end of 1824, and during 1825 Monrovia gained room for five additional communities in surrounding areas. Settlers who wanted to move onto land beyond Monrovia's territory could work out individual agreements with local village chiefs. Land might be purchased with cloth, tools, guns, and other goods. The colonists subsisted on indigenous fruit, vegetables, fish, and wild game and raised livestock such as goats, chickens, and guinea fowls. About four hundred farms produced cotton, corn, indigo, sugar cane, and sorghum for export, while intellectual needs were met by a public library built in 1827 and six public schools in operation by 1830.[22]

One of the chief architects of this early success had little time to enjoy it, as bad health forced Ashmun to leave Liberia and return to the United States where he died on August 28, 1828. The Society's Board of Managers resolved to erect monuments in his memory in his hometown of New Haven, as well as in Monrovia. Before leaving Liberia, Ashmun had appointed Lott Carey, a black Baptist preacher, to take temporary charge of the colony. Carey wrote a friend in Richmond, Virginia lamenting that more colored people had not immigrated to the colony, adding that he believed black people were misinformed about the colony. If one hundred persons were picked off the streets in Richmond and transported to Monrovia, he maintained, not one would wish to return.[23]

Dr. Richard Randall arrived at Monrovia on December 22, 1828 as the new colonial agent. After a few months in Liberia, Randall contracted fever and died the following April, whereupon Dr. Joseph Mechlin, who had accompanied Randall, succeeded to the leadership. Mechlin reported that the colonists were enjoying good health; coffee was beginning to be cultivated and was expected to develop into an important export item, and the commerce of the colony had grown. Fifty-nine vessels had traded in its port, including thirty-two American ships, the remainder being British and French. These merchantmen carried away camwood, ivory, palm oil, tortoise shells and gold, even as the colony nurtured a growing trade with the interior as well.[24]

As the fledging colony increased in size and population, colonizationists in the United States began speaking about a new expanding
American empire in Africa. John H. B. Latrobe, a colonizationist and
Baltimore shipper who saw profits in an expanding colony, requested
that the Board of Managers annex to Liberia the settlements at Cape
Palmas and the island of Bulama. Both of these would allow for population growth and would give Liberia control of the commercial trade from
the interior of Africa. Latrobe hoped that Liberia would also eventually
annex Sierra Leone. He further emphasized that a larger Liberia would
draw additional black immigration from the United States.[25] In several
articles the *African Repository* stressed the vision of a growing empire in
Africa. The light of civilization came to the West from the East, it was
argued, and now the West would return it to the East. The projected empire would bring civilization, Christianity, and prosperity to Africa, and
while the people of the present generation might not live to see all these
benefits, their children surely would.[26]

The vision whether illumined by profits or less mercenary motives,
found growing support in the United Sates. Many of the advocates of
Cape Mesurado's expansion stood to gain from trade with Liberia as
merchants and shippers. Baltimore's John Latrobe and the New York
shipper Arthur Tappan, both supported colonization, and Tappan had
privately sought guarantees for a trading route to Liberia. The fact-
finding mission of Samuel Mills and Ebenezer Burgess in 1817 had been
underwritten by auxiliaries supported by merchants, shippers, and bankers in the commercial centers of Philadelphia, New York, and Baltimore.
Judge Samuel Wilkeson, a colonizationist from New York, wrote to
Lewis Sherridan, a free and successful Northern black farmer, about the
economic advantages of colonization. Wilkeson acknowledged that
blacks were just as capable of becoming skilled workmen as whites.
White prejudices, he thought, would be lessened if an active trade developed in which both planters and merchants could see profits. He suggested that Sherridan organize a ship line to Liberia where a trade would
develop between Liberia and America. Wilkeson would supply the
needed loans for this enterprise. Wilkeson's action again illustrates the
close connection between trade and colonization. Some Americans believed in helping themselves as they helped others. Commercial advantages clearly joined the array of motives behind the establishment and
expansion of the colony at Cape Mesurado.[27]

Colonizationists also argued that the larger Liberia grew, the greater
would be the demand for products which black settlers required. This

market for tobacco and building materials such as nails, iron, and lumber would be supplied by American merchants. The colony would also trade with Sierra Leone which had been closed to American shippers and merchants. From the colony, products like ivory, gold, camwood, palm oil, and beeswax would also be sent to the United States. Ship captains, such as W. A. Weaver, argued for colonization because of the trade benefits it offered. The North could sell its surplus goods while the South could sell its tobacco and secure an outlet for resettling its population of free blacks. A report submitted to the Virginia legislature recommended that state funds be appropriated to support colonization, and merchants, the report argued, would increase their tobacco trade.[28] President Eliphalet Nott of Union College in Schenectady, New York, lent the prestige of academic sanction to colonization in an address to his state's Colonization Society. He endorsed both the practicality and the expediency of colonization, pointing out that many countries such as Greece, Italy, and the United States had begun as colonies. Certainly the settlers at Mesurado had experienced numerous difficulties, but the Pilgrims had also been forced to contend with similar problems in laying the foundations of New England society at Plymouth. Africa, through colonization, would be exposed to the sciences and arts which could help it to become a prosperous continent. With such certain benefits sure to grace free blacks in Liberia, Nott concluded, "Why then in the name of God, should we hesitate to encourage their departure."[29]

Colonizationists reprinted letters from ship captains reporting glowingly about the condition of the Liberia colony. Captain W. E. Sherman, who transported immigrants to the colony, described Monrovia as consisting of ninety houses, various stores, churches, and a council house. The colony enjoyed the protection of a militia consisting of one thousand men. Townships near Monrovia, Caldwell and Millsburg, counted populations of five hundred and two hundred, respectively.

Captain William Abels of the *Margaret Mercer*, a brig owned by the Colonization Society to transport emigrants, told of the thirteen days which he spent in Liberia. He found all the colonists to be in good health, intelligent, well mannered, and well dressed. Abels claimed that not one person he talked with expressed any discontent or any desire to return to America. Both Sherman and Abels, of course, earned their profits by transporting black colonists to Liberia.[30]

In an official report to the Secretary of the Navy concerning the state of the colony, Captain Nicholson of the U.S.S. *Potomac* described Monrovia as having a good harbor which could be easily fortified.[31] About seventy vessels traded annually at Monrovia, and of these, one third were American. The population numbered approximately one thousand persons, and schools in the various settlements were well attended. Cattle and vegetables flourished in abundance. In his opinion the colony had taken root in Africa and would continue to grow. Through letters such as these, colonizationists kept the public informed about the health of the colony.

To lend further credence to the viability of African colonization, the Society published letters from residents of Monrovia addressed to the black population in the United States. The letters, written in response to stories circulated among American blacks describing the great hardships in Africa, claimed that Liberia actually enjoyed all the basic liberties of citizenship, political participation, and land ownership denied them in the United States. Further they enjoyed good health, good schools and homes, various occupations, and all the comforts of life. Most importantly, they claimed, they were not treated as inferiors.[32]

By 1836 Liberia had a population of about three thousand people. Monrovia alone contained about five hundred houses, many built of stone. Docks, public offices, and a light house had also been constructed along with ten church buildings. The territory along the coast stretched about two hundred miles, pushed nearly thirty miles inland, and contained about 200,000 native Africans.[33]

For a variety of reasons a number of colonies sprang up outside Liberia's borders. Between 1830 and 1840 the Maryland, Pennsylvania, New York, Mississippi, and Louisiana state societies established colonies near Liberia under their own policies and directions. Confusion often ensued over jurisdictions and policies between the new colonies and Monrovia. The conflicting parties finally created a commonwealth, forming a union of these colonies with Liberia. Only the settlement of "Maryland in Liberia" remained apart.[34]

Apart from such political difficulties, economic obstacles also restricted Liberia's development. For some eight years Liberia had faced serious problems created by the refusal of British traders from Sierra Leone to accept its commercial regulations and duties. These traders argued that since Liberia was the possession of a private association, it could neither exercise nor enjoy the prerogatives of a sovereign entity. Liberia fined and confiscated several British ships for violation of Liberian trade regulations, and in retaliation the British in Sierra Leone threatened to seize Liberian territory. The American Colonization Society, then hamstrung by debt, urged the Liberians to proclaim independence and become a republic.[35]

In 1847 Liberia issued a declaration of independence, adopted a constitution, and proclaimed itself a republic, and the following year elected Joseph Jenkins Roberts, a mulatto born in Virginia, as the first president of the republic. The population of American origin numbered about 4,500. The seal of the new republic used the motto: "The Love of Liberty Brought Us Here," and the new flag took the flag of the United States as its model, displaying one star in the upper left corner representing Liberia. Eleven alternating bars of red and white represented the number of persons who signed Liberia's Declaration of Independence.[36] Great Britain and France quickly recognized the new republic, but the United States withheld official recognition until 1862 because of the slavery controversy.[37]

Even after Liberia had declared its independence in 1847, the Colonization Society continued to transport free blacks to Liberia. From 1848 to 1854 the Society chartered forty-one ships and sent four thousand black settlers to Liberia. In 1856 the Society built its own emigrant ship, the *Mary Caroline Stevens* which made dozens of trips from Liberia before the outbreak of the Civil War.

All told, from 1820 to 1860 10,517 blacks immigrated to Liberia.[38] Some of these immigrants were free blacks living in the North who contacted the Colonization Society requesting transportation to Liberia. Marville H. Smith, a free black writing on behalf of a group of fellow blacks living in Illinois, requested permission from the national Society to immigrate to Liberia. "We are ready to start from Shawneetown at any moment, and wish to come as soon as possible, for though we are free in name we are not free in fact," Smith lamented. "We are in as bad, or worse condition than the slaves of which you speak," he added, "being compelled to leave the state, or give security, and those of the whites who would befriend us are debarred by the fear of public opinion." Black people, Smith continued, were often punished for crimes they had not committed, and he concluded that their present condition was "worse than slavery."[39]

Most blacks who emigrated, however, were slaves released by their owners on the condition that they be transported to Liberia. Robert Cox in his will emancipated thirty-six slaves and left them several hundred dollars to help defray the cost of deportation.[40] A Mr. Funston of Frederick County, Virginia in his will emancipated ten slaves and provided $1,000 to cover their transportation costs to Liberia. William Fletcher of

North Carolina manumitted his slaves who were then to be hired for a year in order to raise the necessary funds to transport them to Liberia.[41] Williams B. Lynch of Virginia emancipated and transported eighteen slaves to Liberia, providing five hundred dollars toward the transportation costs and furnishing them with clothing and agricultural implements.[42] The *African Repository* was replete with such stories, suggesting how widespread was the practice of slave owners releasing their slaves and paying transportation costs to Liberia.

The Society's official organ also offered various schemes detailing how slave owners could release their slaves on condition of migration to Liberia and yet meet the bondsmens' transportation expenses without cost to themselves. John McDonogh of New Orleans presented a plan to emancipate and transport his own slaves to Liberia, offering his slaves a chance to earn their freedom by paying them for the work they did between mid-day and midnight on Saturday. McDonogh maintained that other slave owners could do the same, estimating that it would take fourteen to fifteen years for these slaves to pay their way to Liberia.[43] Allowing the slaves to earn their freedom offered a solution, however strained, to the vexing problem of financing colonization. Many articles bemoaned the Society's lack of friends who would finance black immigration to Liberia; Elliott Cressons claimed that nearly two thousand applicants for colonization awaited the funds necessary for their transportation. He maintained that James Monroe estimated that if funds were available "he could procure 10,000 slaves by voluntary emancipation in his native state alone."[44] The scarcity of financial resources, however, helped insure that the number of immigrants to Liberia would be small.

While Liberia became an independent state in 1847, it continued to rely upon support from the American Colonization Society well beyond the Civil War. But by the 1840s, both the Society and its African colony receded from its formerly preeminent role in the debate over American slavery. Some northern moralists had grown critical of the Society, arguing that it was more harmful then helpful to blacks residing in the United States. These critics parted from the likes of Robert Finley, Elias Caldwell, and Henry Clay, insisting upon black freedom and acceptance in the New World. After all, they argued, these Africans were as much citizens of the Western Hemisphere as those white Americans whose heritage was rooted in Europe.

NOTES

1. For an explanation of the government's unwillingness to support colonization, refer to chapter 2.

2. Richard West, *Back to Africa: A History of Sierra Leone and Liberia* (London: Jonathan Cape, 1970), 101-102; Staudenraus, *African Colonization*, 37-41.

3. Staudenraus, *African Colonization*, 41.

4. *Ibid.*, 43.

5. An Act in addition to the acts prohibiting the Slave Trade, March 3, 1819, *Annuals of Congress* 32: 2544-2546.

6. Charles Francis Adams, ed. *Memoirs of John Quincy Adams, Comprising Portions of His Diary From 1795 to 1848* (Philadelphia: J.B. Lippincott & Co., 1875), 4: 292-294.

7. Special Message, December 17, 1819, James D. Richardson, *A Compilation of the Messages and Papers of the Presidents* (20 vols., New York: Bureau of National Literature, 1897), 2: 633-634.

8. Veto Message, May 4, 1822, *ibid.*, 712; W. P. Cresson, *James Monroe* (Chapel Hill: University of North Carolina Press, 1946), 340; Harry Ammon, *James Monroe: The Quest for National Identity* (New York: McGraw-Hill Book Company, 1917), 522-523.

9. Charles Marrow Wilson, *Liberia: Black Africa in Microcosm* (New York: Harper and Row, 1971), 17-18.

10. Martin Lowenkopf, *Politics of Liberia: The Conservative Road to Development* (Stanford: Hoover Institution Press, 1976), 12-13.

11. Wilson, *Liberia*, 19-20.

12. West, *Back to Africa*, 113; Morrow, *Liberia*, 15; Lowenkopf, *Politics in Liberia*, 31; Yekutiel Gershoni, *Black Colonialism: The Americo-Liberian Scramble for the Hinterland* (Boulder: Westview Press, 1985), 204.

13. Fox, *American Colonization Society*, 67-68; West *Back to Africa*, 115; A copy of the deed which King Peter and the other tribal chiefs signed ceding the land to Stockton and Ayres is found in Alexander, *History of Colonization*, 172-174.

14. Fox, *American Colonization Society*, 67-68; Alexander, *History of Colonization*, 167-173.

15. Galbraith Welch, *The Jet Lighthouse*, (London: Museum Press Limited, 1960), 195-196; Jehudi Ashmun, *History of the American Colony in Liberia from 1821 to 1823*, (Washington: Way and Gideon, 1826), 7-14.

16. Ralph Randolph Gurley, *Life of Jehudi Ashmun, Late Colonial Agent in Liberia*, (New York: Robinson and Franklin, 1839; reprint, Freeport: Books For Library Press, 1971), 18-26, 29, 55-61.

17. Staudenraus, *African Colonization*, 88.

18. West, *Back to Africa*, 121-123; Alexander, *History of Colonization*, 178-197; Staudenraus, *African Colonization,* 87-89.

19. Alexander, *History of Colonization*, 204, 208-219; Staudenraus, *African Colonization*, 91-97.

20. Harper's speech to the Colonization Society as recorded in Alexander, *History to Colonization*, 232; Staudenraus, *African Colonization*, 39.

21. Staudenraus, *African Colonization*, 155-156; Alexander, *History of Colonization*, 220-221.

22. Wilson, *Liberia*, 36-39, 41.

23. "Testimony of Colonists," *African Repository*, 3 (October, 1817): 249.

24. Alexander, *History of Colonization*, 374-378.

25. "Annual Meeting of the American Colonization Society," *African Repository* 3 (January, 1828): 325-331.

26. "Annual Meeting of Auxiliary Societies," *African Repository* 1 (January, 1826): 337-347; "Annual Meeting of the American Colonization Society," *African Repository* 2 (January, 1827): 33; "Park's Testimony in favor of the possibility of Civilizing the Africans," *African Repository* 4 (May, 1828): 76-77.

27. Staudenraus, *African Colonization*, 157-163. "New and Interesting Project," *African Repository* 14 (February, 1838): 58-60.

28. "Important Intelligence from Liberia," *African Repository* 2 (November, 1826): 270-271; "Report submitted to the Legislature of Virginia," *African Repository* 3 (January, 1828): 346-347; "Capt. Weaver's Letter in regard to the Colony," *African Repository* 7 (January, 1832): 341-342.

29. "Proceedings on the Formation of the New York State Colonization Society," *African Repository* 5 (November, 1829): 273-279.

30. Sherman to Edward Hallowell, May 10, 1830, in Alexander, *History of Colonization*, 342-344; Abels as cited, *ibid.*, 367-368.

31. Nicholson to the Secretary of the Navy, in Alexander, *History of Colonization*, 540-543.

32. Address, August 27, 1827, in Alexander, *History of Colonization*, 287-293, 529. A similar letter was written again in 1837.

33. *Ibid.*, 513.

34. Staudenraus, *African Colonization*, 240-241.

35. *Ibid.*

36. Benjamin Brawley, *A Social History of the American Negro* (New York: The MacMillan Company, 1921), 190-191.

37. Lowenkopf, *Politics in Liberia*, 19-20.

38. Staudenraus, *African Colonization*, 251.

39. "An Appeal," *African Repository* 18 (July, 1842): 220-221.

40. "Manumissions," *ibid.*, 3 (March, 1827): 27.

41. "Manumissions," *ibid.*, 2 (January, 1827): 352-353.

42. "Annual Meeting of the Massachusetts Colonization Society, July, 1843," *ibid.*, 19 (December, 1842): 301.

43. "A Letter of John McDonogh on African Colonization," *African Repository* 19 (July, 1842): 48-60, 141-142.

44. "What Can Colonization Do?" *African Repository* 15 (March, 1839): 84.

Chapter 4
Riveting the Chains of Slavery

In spite of the fervency of the cause, colonization faced obstacles other than inadequate financial resources. The proponents of gradual emancipation through colonization of freed slaves too often ignored those most fundamentally concerned, the blacks themselves. Former slaves and free blacks proved, on the whole, to be unwilling recruits to the resettlement campaign.

After the Society had submitted its memorial to Congress requesting government support, an anonymous writer criticized this presentation in the *National Intelligencer*. The writer claimed that free blacks were happy in the United States and that "they know no country but that of their birth." Free blacks, the writer insisted, "are free men, and consider themselves in every respect qualified to determine for themselves what is, and what is not for their own benefit and advantage." A better remedy than colonization to Africa was amalgamation. In words certain to shock most contemporary readers, the writer declared that young black men were willing to marry white women. This suggestion may have been intended to stir up hostility through satire. "In a few generations," the writer continued, "the odious distinction of color would pass away, and the posterity of your memorialist would find themselves blended with the great American family."[1]

Spokesmen from the free black community commonly denounced the founding principle of the Colonization Society. Free blacks in Philadelphia meeting in the Bethel Methodist Church resented the designation of free blacks as "a dangerous and useless part of the community." The assemblage passed resolutions rejecting colonization and forwarded them to Joseph Hopkins, the United States Representative for Philadelphia. James Forten, a free black leader in Philadelphia and chairman of this meeting, may have been in favor of colonization. Forten was a close friend of Paul Cuffee, a wealthy black shipper, who transported at his expense thirty-eight blacks from the United States to Sierra Leone in 1815. Forten was interested in this endeavor. After Robert Finley had started the Colonization Society in Washington, he met with Forten and other black leaders in Philadelphia to discuss colonization. Forten did show some interest in the project. However, when the meeting of three thousand blacks took place, Forten wrote Cuffee that "there was not one sole [sic] that was in favor of going to Africa." "My opinion," he added, "is that they com[e] out from amongst the white people, but as the majority is decidedly against me I am determined to remain silent, except as to my opinion which I freely give when asked." However, six months later at another anti-colonization meeting, Forten had abandoned colonization. Forten may also have been instrumental in convincing Garrison, who was a mild colonizationist, to abandon colonization. He helped to collect subscriptions for Garrison's *Liberator* and provided much of the information and funds necessary for Garrison to write and publish *Thoughts on African Colonization.*[2]

Reactions of some blacks to colonization were not completely negative, what they did oppose was colonization to Africa. Free blacks in Richmond, Virginia met and expressed their reaction to the Colonization Society. While not adverse to the idea of colonization itself, they objected to being transported to Africa; they suggested instead a colony somewhere in the United States, perhaps on the Missouri River, as a better alternative.[3]

By the 1830s, however, it appears that most free blacks vehemently opposed colonization. Forty black delegates representing seven states gathered in September, 1830 in Philadelphia's Bethel Methodist Church where they formed the "American Society of Free Persons of Colour." Drawing on the principles of the Declaration of Independence, the convention called upon free blacks to raise their status in society and to fight against slavery. The new organization condemned African colonization along with the Colonization Society for stigmatizing blacks as unfit for citizenship or equality.[4]

As free blacks increasingly turned their attention to the colonization movement, the "First Annual Convention of the People of Color" of June 6-11, 1831 in Philadelphia, discussed the racism pervasive in the United States and the need for a college to educate young blacks. The convention condemned the policy of the Colonization Society, claiming that they would rather "die at home" than be "sacrificed to their [the Society's] philanthropy." The convention members also asserted that since many of their fathers fought and died in the War of Independence, "it would be ungenerous and unfeeling in you to deny us a humble and quiet grave in the country which gave us birth."[5] The organization's second convention, meeting again at Philadelphia in 1832, spoke more vehemently against the Colonization Society, scathingly condemning its aims as

> at enmity with the principles and precepts of religion, humanity, and justice, and should be regarded by every man of color in these United States as an evil, for magnitude, unexcelled, and whose doctrines aim at the entire extinction of the free colored population and the riveting of slavery.[6]

Later meetings convened in cities such as Baltimore, New York, Boston, Brooklyn, Pittsburgh, Willington, Harrisburg, New Haven, Providence, and Trenton. Lewis Tappan claimed that these meetings and "their united and strenuous opposition to the expatriation scheme . . . induced William Lloyd Garrison and others to oppose" colonization.[7] Much of Garrison's *Thoughts of African Colonization* came from and reflected these views expressed by free blacks in the 1820s, but the white Garrison was able to publicize them far more widely than were free blacks.[8]

Most black leaders, such as the escaped slave and abolitionist Frederick Douglass, reviled African colonization, insisting that all blacks should fight for both emancipation and citizenship. After watching the general government remove southern Indians to new locations across the Mississippi, blacks became more alarmed and vocal in their opposition to colonization. They heralded immediate emancipation and racial equality, not colonization, as the answer to both southern slavery and northern prejudice.[9]

William Lloyd Garrison, the New England journalist who dramatically transformed the antislavery movement after 1830, agreed. Garrisonian abolitionism, although a minority movement in the 1830s, provided the strongest and most articulate critique against African colonization. The Colonization Society provided Garrison a focal point to attack slavery and publicize his doctrine of immediatism. Antislavery societies had arisen before Garrison, of course, but their programs favored moderation, and they confined their activities to their respective states where they petitioned their legislatures to end the slave trade and help in "improving the condition of the African race." The first interstate antislavery convention had met in Philadelphia in 1794, with delegates coming mainly from the middle states. They appealed to Congress "that a law may be passed, prohibiting the traffic carried on by citizens of the United States for the supply of slaves," but issued no outright call for the immediate and unconditional abolition of slavery.[10]

Garrison, like many other early antislavery advocates, initially favored colonization. As late as 1829 he delivered the annual Fourth of July colonization address, "Dangers to the Nation," in Boston's Park Street Church. The nation must release itself from the perpetual curse of slavery he declaimed, and blacks must be educated and granted the same freedoms enjoyed by whites. Garrison assured his audience, however, that "the emancipation of all the slaves of this generation is most assuredly out of the question. Years may elapse," Garrison continued, "before the completion of the achievement; generations of blacks may go down to the grave, manacled and lacerated, without hope for their children . . . [,] but the work will go on . . . the victory will be obtained, worth the desperate struggle of a thousands years." Before this victory could be achieved, however, much work needed doing. Garrison concluded by summoning different members of society, notably church leaders and editors, to keep this ultimate hope of victory constantly in the public mind. Finally, casting his lot with the expatriationists, Garrison pleaded, "I call upon our citizens to assist in establishing auxiliary colonization societies in every state, county, and town. I implore their direct and liberal patronage to the parent society."[11]

Eventually, however, Garrison would reevaluate his position on emancipation and colonization after joining Benjamin Lundy in 1829 as coeditor of the *Genius of Universal Emancipation*. Garrison came to reject gradualism for the more radical goal of immediate abolition after a period of intense study and reflection. Garrison's change from gradual to immediate emancipation may have come from his reading of British antislavery literature. Garrison read this literature along with speeches given in Parliament for the immediate emancipation of slaves in the British West Indies.[12] His conversion came decisively and abruptly and led him into abrasive attacks against the slave trade. Garrison began to reflect the aggressive style of British abolitionism in his own campaign against slavery. This new aggressiveness prompted several criminal and civil libel suits, and these soon brought an end to his partnership with Lundy, who favored gradual emancipation combined with colonization. Lundy discontinued publishing the *Genius* on a weekly basis and began to publish a monthly edition instead. In the final weekly editorial, he indicated that financial reasons dictated such a change; subscribers simply were not paying their dues. Also Garrison would no longer be coeditor. Garrison's sharp attacks against slavery and the libel suits brought against him had hurt the paper. Even so, Lundy stated that though some of Garrison's articles "did not entirely meet my approbation," he and Garrison still had "the kindliest feelings and mutual personal regard."[13] Garrison assured his readers that his leaving the paper presaged no slackening of his anti-slavery crusade: "Every pledge, however, that I have made to the public shall be fulfilled. My pen cannot remain idle, nor my voice be suppressed, nor my heart cease to bleed, while two millions of my fellow-beings wear the shackles of slavery in my own guilty country." Garrison made this promise in the *Genius'* final weekly editorial following Lundy's editorial.[14]

While Garrison did not inaugurate opposition to slavery, he did alter it dramatically. Abolition, while still a minority movement, became more fervent and intractable under his prodding. The increased profitability of cotton's slave-driven economy coupled with the abolitions' implacability drove the movement from the South. In Garrison's strident and moralistic rhetoric, slavery was a sin, and Christians must not in any manner compromise with it. Garrison branded slave owners as "incorrigible sinners" as well as "greedy and relentless robbers" who must "Repent! Repent! Now, in sackcloth and ashes."[15] Abolitionists such as Garrison employed biblical imagery in describing the system of slavery, and the abolitionist agent became a traveling revivalist exhorting all to cast off the depraved practice of human bondage. Abolitionists of Garrison's ilk demanded that people consider slavery fundamentally as iniquity towards God, repent of this wickedness, and abolish it immediately.[16]

Many of the key movers involved in militant abolitionism had matured in strong religious environments. Garrison had been reared a Baptist, Theodore Dwight Weld, an equally prominent figure, was the son of a minister and attended Lane Theological Seminary, Arthur and Lewis Tappan, wealthy New York silk merchants, became revivalists through the preaching of Charles Finney, while Gerrit Smith grew up in a religious family and attended revivals in the early 1830s. Although these militant abolitionists enjoyed such backgrounds, most northern antislavery Protestants supported gradual emancipation with colonization rather than immediate abolition. Similarly, militant abolitionist clergymen made up only a small percentage of the whole clergy. Garrison grew disgusted with most churches for not taking a more aggressive stand against slavery. James G. Birney labeled churches as "the bulwarks of American slavery." He turned from religious sentiment to political action when he ran against James K. Polk and Henry Clay for the presidency in 1844 as candidate of the Liberty Party. Many diehard abolitionists of the Garrisonian brand deliberately distanced themselves from formal religion in an attempt to push the movement into a secular channel, but Garrison and others like him never eased their religious thrust.[17]

Like the peripatetic evangelists of his era, Garrison moved through various cities and then to Boston speaking out against slavery while looking for work. In 1831 he launched *The Liberator*, a small weekly paper which initially claimed a predominantly black readership. The journal appealed to free blacks in Boston by praising black accomplishments and defending black claims to citizenship. The first edition of the *Liberator* appeared on January 1, 1831, marked by the intransigent and abrasive language and tone which would typify its tenure:

> I am aware, that many object to the severity of my language; but is there not cause for severity? I will be as harsh as truth, and as uncompromising as justice. In this subject, I do not wish to think, or speak, or write, with moderation. No! No! tell a man whose house is on fire, to give moderate alarm; tell him to moderately rescue his wife from the hands of the ravisher; tell the mother to gradually extricate her babe from the fire into which it has fallen; but urge me not to use moderation in a cause like the present. I am in earnest–I will not equivocate–I will not excuse–I will not retreat a single inch–and I will be heard.[18]

Garrison reserved much of his vituperation for the Colonization Society, warning his readers: "Let us, at once, abandon the wild, destructive, unnatural scheme of colonization." He blatantly accused the Society for perpetrating slavery and of being "the apologist for slave owners."[19]

In 1832 Garrison collated many of his abolitionist ideas into *Thoughts of African Colonization*, a book which dismissed the Society as "a creature without heart, without brains, eyeless, unnatural, hypocritical, relentless, and unjust." Garrison charged the Society with persecution of blacks because it transported them out of their country and discouraged them from improving their condition and education in their native land. Colonization, Garrison warned, "is lulling the country into a fatal sleep."[20] Furthermore, the movement was no less than "a libel upon republicanism–a libel upon the Declaration of Independence–a libel upon Christianity." It only encouraged and perpetuated slavery by taking away the reproaches and assuaging the guilt of owning slaves. The Society was the slave owner's "devoted servant," Garrison charged.[21] Garrison relentlessly attacked colonization, and ministers who supported the venture or refused to speak out against slavery he labeled as "madmen or atheists."[22]

Yet even Garrison in his implacable hostility toward slavery and its supporters drew back from absolute freedom from blacks. Garrison defined abolition as the end of the slave trade, the whip, separated families, and stolen wages. Yet his view "immediate abolition does not mean that the slaves shall immediately exercise the right of suffrage, or be eligible of any office, or be emancipated from law, or be free from the benevolent restraints of guardianship." Garrison envisioned for freed slaves an evolutionary path initialized by access to education and opportunity to pursue all trades and employments. Free blacks would be no nuisance or threat to white society, Garrison assured his readers. They would instead, become friends and more effective workers since they would be laboring for themselves.[23]

To achieve this perceived partnership, whites must begin by refusing to buy products made by slaves, encouraging planters to use free laborers to cultivate their fields, educating blacks, and by "constantly exhibiting the criminality of holding rational and immortal beings in servile bondage."[24] In this scenario Garrison did offer one possible role for the Colonization Society. Should the Society seek immediate abolition, expose the guilt of slave owners, fight for equal rights for blacks, and pursue the end of racial prejudice, then Garrison declared unequivocally, "my opposition to it would cease."[25]

The Colonization Society initially reacted reservedly to Garrison's proposals. By ignoring his attacks, the Society hoped to blunt the Garrisonian critique of their venture. Garrison, however, persisted in exposing the alleged weakness of colonization. In January, 1831, he led in the creation of the New England Anti-Slavery Society which launched its attack by sending speakers from Boston into nearby cities and towns to promulgate the anti-colonization doctrine. The colonizationists, still enjoying a monopoly in the antislavery campaign, continued to ignore these charges. The new Society initially garnered few members and often appealed at first only to black audiences. As more whites, however, came to lend a serious ear to abolitionists' arguments against colonization and as Garrison's societies sprang up in several cities, colonizationists became alarmed.

To add to its troubles, by the end of 1833 the Colonization Society had accumulated a deficit. Part of this shortfall resulted from declining contributions as a result of abolitionist attacks. In futile desperation some colonizationists supported mob violence against the militant abolitionists, although no concrete evidence points to the Society itself as instigating or organizing anti-abolitionist violence. In New York City, a colonization stronghold, organizers cancelled an abolitionist meeting scheduled for Clinton Hall on October 3, 1833 when a mob, including many colonizationists, surrounded the building. The rabble then destroyed several black homes and three black churches. Again in New York City in July, 1834 crowds thronged the streets shouting their support for colonization. In October, 1835 a mob interlaced with prominent citizens, broke up a convention of the New York State Anti-Slavery Society at Utica. Many members of the mob who killed the abolitionist editor, Elijah Lovejoy, at Alton, Illinois in 1837 openly supported colonization, although such support had, no doubt, more to do with the perceived economic and racial threat posed by a large free black presence than with the desire for gradual emancipation.

Abolitionists, moreover, threatened the alliance of the cotton interests in both sections of the country. The disruption of the Union would hurt the economic interests of the "lords of the loom," whose textile mills fed on southern cotton. Prominent colonizationists, including doctors, merchants, bankers, and judges, often supported gradual abolition by organizing anti-abolition mob actions to promote colonization as a means of ending slavery. At the same time, these men of eminence also sought to protect their own authority they enjoyed as local elites. The militant abolitionists, on the other hand, sought to influence the people directly through mass meetings and free literature advocating immediate emancipation, thereby circumventing local politicians who might have opposed their cause.[26] Despite the best efforts of the "gentlemen of property and standing," the movement for immediate abolition grew. Much of this growth resulted because militant abolitionists were far more effective in promoting their viewpoint than were colonizationists.

While the Colonization Society depended upon traveling agents to promote their goals, the militant abolitionists relied more heavily upon the printed word. They cast a blizzard of immediate abolitionist pamphlets and tracts on cheap paper and distributed them widely free of charge. These pamphlets and tracts appeared in the reading rooms of many colleges and seminaries; copies moved through the mail to New England editors and clergymen. The Society, in contradistinction issued only a few pamphlets, normally printed on more expensive paper and selling for twelve to twenty-five cents each, making distribution difficult. The *African Repository*, the Colonization Society's official journal, never counted more than five thousand subscribers. Much of the Society's income went toward payment for traveling agents and the defraying of colonization expenses rather than for printing.[27]

Through their adeptness at publicity the immediate abolitionists, while still in the minority, threw the colonizationists, with their more nationally appealing proposals, into crisis. While many in New England viewed Garrison as a radical, others increasingly harbored serious doubts about colonization. Students at Princeton College, where Finley had received his early support for forming the American Colonization Society, abandoned colonization in favor of immediate abolition. At Western Reserve College in Hudson, Ohio, both students and professors turned forcefully to militant abolitionism.[28]

Garrison's critique was, moreover, impacting key supporters of African colonization. Arthur Tappan, a wealthy New York City merchant and an early supporter of colonization, renounced colonization on two grounds. First, he could not reconcile sending alcohol, gunpowder, and weapons to the colony at Liberia with the Society's professed missionary goals. Second, he claimed that he had joined the Society believing that it would end slavery and help evangelize Africa, but after reading Garrison's abolitionist articles, he now believed that the Society was "a device of Satan, to rivet still closer the fetters of the slaves, and to deepen the prejudice against the free colored people."[29] Tappan liberally supported Garrison's *Liberator*, purchasing large numbers of the paper and distributing them to various individuals and institutions, including Lane Seminary and Western Reserve College.[30] In 1833 he became president of the New York City Anti-Slavery Society, and late that year the American Anti-Slavery Society in New York City named Tappan as its head.[31]

Theodore Weld as late as 1832 still held to colonization as the only way to end slavery. Writing to James G. Birney, Weld maintained: "I am ripe in the conviction that if the Colonization Society does not dissipate the horror of darkness which overhangs the southern country, we are undone. Light breaks in from no other quarter."[32] The efforts, however, of British abolitionist Charles Stuart and a group of Western Reserve College faculty and students who were now active Garrisonians, soon converted Weld to immediate abolitionism.[33] Again writing to Birney in 1834, Weld claimed that colonization

keeps in existence and renders more and more these very disabilities, outrages and wrongs from which it purposes to relieve the colored man only by throwing him out of their reach when it is perfectly in the power of society to change public sentiment and thus remove the necessity of colonizing which it has always alleged. I have dwelt on this

point dear brother because it is a consideration which most powerfully
sways my own mind.[34]

Weld was able to convince most of the student body at Lane Seminary to
embrace immediate abolition. In response the seminary, whose faculty
and board of trustees advocated colonization, prohibited debates on slavery and dissolved the antislavery society formed on its campus. Many of
the students then left Lane Seminary, including Weld who never finished
his training. He launched into ardent advocacy of immediate abolition
speaking in hundreds of locales and establishing numerous immediate
abolitionist societies in Ohio, a colonizationist stronghold.[35]
     Weld also played an instrumental role in convincing Birney to re-
nounce colonization and lend his support for immediate abolition. Birney, himself a slave owner, was appointed by the Colonization Society in
1832 as its agent in Alabama, Mississippi, Louisiana, Arkansas, and
Tennessee.[36] Birney also published a series of seven colonizationists'
essays in the Alabama *Huntsville Democrat* which were reprinted in the
African Repository.[37] Writing entirely for a southern slave owning audience, Birney argued that transporting free blacks to Africa would reduce
serious threats of insurrections, thus promoting better behavior among
the slaves. This, he hoped would, in turn, encourage slave owners voluntarily and gradually to manumit their slaves. Birney admired colonization
as a viable method of freeing slaves without creating a direct threat to
those slave owners who shrank at the prospect of a large free black population.
     Birney and Weld corresponded frequently, discussing colonization
and immediate abolition. In 1834 Birney visited Weld at Lane Seminary
and shortly thereafter resigned his agency and renounced colonization in
favor of immediate abolition. Writing to Gerrit Smith, a close friend and
a colonizationist, Birney lamented that it was "the total failure of gradualism to lay hold of men's consciences that must ever render it ineffec-
tual for the extermination of slavery in our country." Birney was convinced that the "only way of getting rid of this great disgrace of our
Church and our country, is, to urge, with all truth and firmness and fair-
ness, its sinfulness." Consequently, immediate abolition needs to be
preached and practiced. To preach and practice gradual abolition would
"be as inefficient as would be the preaching of gradual and partial repen-
tance toward God," a concept both Birney and Smith would find repul-
sive.[38] Later, antislavery presses publicized Birney's conversion by printing and disturbing copies of his *A Letter on Colonization*, formally re-

nouncing colonization. Birney's letter was first published in the Lexington *Western Luminary* beginning July 15, 1834. Later it was published as a pamphlet by the American Anti-Slavery Society.[39]

While Garrison's critique of colonization as a method of emancipation apparently had no great impact upon the general public, it did cause prominent men like Arthur and Lewis Tappan, Gerrit Smith, Theodore Weld, and James Birney to abandon colonization in favor of immediate abolition. Many of these men became ardent abolitionists and helped to promote and publicize the abolition movement. The withdrawal of support by such influential men as Tappan and Smith, compounded the woes of the Colonization Society by detracting from its popularity and diminishing its financial resources in the 1830s and 1840s. Gerrit Smith may have been one of the Colonization Society's biggest contributors. In 1828 he developed what was later called the Gerrit Smith Plan. Supporters of the Society, including himself, would contribute $100 a year for ten years. This plan raised $54,000. Years later, in 1834, when the Society was experiencing financial difficulties, Smith proposed a similar plan. He pledged $5,000 if other colonization supporters were willing to pledge $100 apiece in order to raise $50,000. This plan was aborted as the necessary pledges were not raised. However, Smith did contribute the $5,000 he pledged.[40]

Garrison's attacks against colonization also helped to define the major focus of the slavery issue: the thorny question of race relations. Slave owners and their supporters held to their dogma that the races were unequal. Even the majority of Americans who questioned the validity of slavery had reservations about giving blacks equal rights with whites. Blacks and whites could not coexist, many thought, in a "biracial society." Colonizationists reflected and reinforced these assumptions. They saw themselves as a conservative, evolutionary reform movement offering a practical solution to a difficult issue. Emancipation, therefore, must be gradual, followed by colonization to Africa.

Militant abolitionists professed, to the contrary, support for the principle of racial egalitarianism. These abolitionists consequently demanded the immediate, unconditional release of slaves and the freedman's full integration into white society. They would brook no compromise for this goal, which they pursued with a religious and moral zeal. Educating and giving blacks equal access to employment opportunities militant abolitionist deemed essential to their program.[41] Most Americans, who favored the more moderate colonization program, judged this agenda too radical.

The clash between the colonizationists and the militant abolitionists particularly exacerbated tensions between the North and South. Henry Clay, both a slave owner himself and an ardent colonizationist, well understood the danger posed by slavery to the preservation of the Union. Southern slaveholding interests embraced their "peculiar institution" as the very cornerstone of their economy and society, yet Clay knew also that for many Americans, including some southerners, slavery posed both an economic and a moral dilemma. Consequently, Clay, "the great compromiser" who had skillfully alleviated bitter sectional differences by working out political deals such as the Missouri Compromise (1820), the Compromise Tariff (1833), and the Compromise of 1850, professed colonization as a moderate compromise between two dangerous extremes.

Speaking to the United States Senate in 1839 at the peak of the conflict between colonizationists and militant abolitionists, Clay charged the abolitionists with encouraging disunion and sectional conflict. These partisans, Clay warned, by putting pressure on Congress for immediate emancipation, were ignoring property rights and the power of the states that alone had the authority to deal with the issue of slavery: "A single idea has taken possession of their minds, and onward they pursue it, overlooking all barriers, reckless, and regardless of all consequences." If these abolitionists succeed in the North, then the only alternative for the South would be "a clash of arms." Clay foresaw not only disunion and civil war, but also a race war between whites and blacks as a result of immediate emancipation. Clay apparently reflected one of the great fears that troubled southerners concerning immediatism, especially in the lower South where in some counties blacks outnumbered whites.[42]

Clay also reflected the anxieties of conservative northerners as well. Boston's Harrison Gray Otis warned that immediate abolitionism would result in disunion and civil war; should the free states agitate for a general emancipation enactment, then the Union would fracture. Southerners would interpret all measures of emancipation as acts of war threatening their properties, economic existence, and way of life. Otis also charged abolitionists with hostility to the spirit and letter of the Constitution which was made and ratified by the people of the states in full acknowledgement of the existence of slavery. The federal government held no right of jurisdiction over Dixie's "peculiar institution."[43] South Carolina, the architect of nullification in 1832, took the lead in propounding this view. During the nullification crisis, South Carolina had maintained that if the federal government could supersede the Constitution in the matter of tariff regulation, it could also do the same with respect to slavery.[44]

Faced with mounting militant abolitionist pressure, yet flush with unprecedented slave-driven prosperity, the South heightened its defense of slavery as a "positive good." As petitions poured into Congress from abolitionists, the South responded by pushing through the House of Representatives the so-called gag rule which decreed the tabling of all anti-slavery appeals without debate. The preamble and resolution read as follows:

> And whereas it is extremely important and desirable that the agitation of this subject should be finally arrested, for the purpose of restoring tranquility to the public mind, your committee respectfully recommends the adoption of the following additional resolution, viz: Resolved, that all petitions, memorials, resolutions, propositions, or papers, relating in any way, or to any extent whatever, to the subject of slavery, or the abolition of slavery, shall, without being either printed or referred, be laid upon the table, and that no further action whatever shall be had thereon.

The resolution was adopted 117 to 68.[45] John Quincy Adams, who would lead an eight year fight to repeal the gag rule, spoke out against the resolution on the House floor after the vote was counted: "I hold the resolution to be direct violation of the constitution of the United States, the rules of this House, and the rights of my constituents."[46] The gag rule coupled with the southern states' censorship of their mail added fuel to the fire of the abolitionist charge that a slave power conspiracy threatened to stifle civil liberties in the nation. The issue at stake, they contended, was no longer merely black freedom, but white freedom as well.

The Deep South, of course, had never been enamored by colonization. Few colonization societies existed in South Carolina and Georgia, although in 1819 local colonization auxiliaries were founded in cities such as Augusta, Savannah, Fayetteville, Raleigh, and Chapel Hill. They soon faded, however, especially when the slavery issue sprang to life with Missouri's admission into the Union, and the cotton gin soon made feasible the remarkable spread and prosperity of short staple cotton. On February 18, 1825, Rufus King of New York submitted a resolution to the Senate promoting colonization. Under his plan, once the public debt had been paid, funds from the sale of public lands would be applied toward emancipating and colonizing slaves with the states' approval; willing free blacks might also be colonized. South Carolina adamantly op-

posed all federal assistance to African colonization, and ten days later
that state's Robert Y. Hayne submitted a resolution to the Senate declaring that Congress had no power to appropriate money for either emancipation or colonization. For Congress to do so "would be a departure from
the condition and spirit of the compact between the several States; and . .
. [these] measures would be calculated to disturb the peace and harmony
of the Union."[47] Again in 1827 a memorial to Congress requested national aid for African colonization, and once again Hayne spoke out
against federal involvement in colonization claiming of the scheme: "I
know of none more wild, impracticable, or mischievous, than this of
colonization."[48] Another South Carolinian, Robert James Turnbull, al-
luded to King's resolution, by arguing that for Congress to purchase
slaves and transport them to Africa would have the effect "of altering the
Constitution of the United States" because slave states would thereby
lose their three-fifths slave representation in Congress. Should such an
amendment be added to the Constitution, the states who opposed it had
the right to dissolve the compact made in forming the Union.[49]

Considering South Carolina's adamant opposition to African colonization, it is difficult to envision colonization as a workable solution to
slavery in the Deep South. Colonization carried more appeal and support
in the border slave states such as Maryland where slavery was not as
profitable as in the cotton kingdom further south. The Upper South, instead, willingly endorsed the colonization movement as a means of ridding itself of free blacks and gradually ending slavery.

As the sectional crisis intensified in the 1850s, many concerned un-
ionists upheld colonization as a moderate alternative to disunion.[50] While
colonization enjoyed virtually no appeal in the Deep South, the Upper
South strongly supported it. Colonization may have been important in
drawing some of the Upper South to the Union when the Civil War broke
out in 1861. Frederick Bancroft, in his essay on African colonization,
suggested that "the adoption of any system of compensated emancipation
might at least have prevented the Civil War from being as serious as it
was, by restricting secession to six or eight states. That would have been
a great gain."[51]

NOTES

1. "A Counter-Memorial proposed to be submitted to Congress in behalf of the free people of colour of the District of Columbia," *National Intelligencer*, 4 (December 30, 1816): 3.

2. James Forten to Paul Cuffee, January 25, 1817, quoted by William Loren Katz, "Earliest Responses of American Negroes and Whites to African Colonization," foreword in Garrison, *Thoughts on African Colonization*, i-xi; Brown, *Robert Finley*, 122-124; James Forten to William Lloyd Garrison, December 31, 1830, and May 6, 1832, *The Black Abolitionist Papers*, C. Peter Ripley, ed. (Chapel Hill: The University of North Carolina Press, 1991), 3: 85-91.

3. Louis R. Mehlinger, "The Attitude of the Free Black Negro toward African Colonization," *Journal of Negro History* 1 (July 1916): 276-301.

4. Bella Gross, "The First National Negro Convention," *Journal of Negro History* 31 (October 1946): 435-443.

5. George W. Williams, *History of the Negro Race in America, 1618-1880* (New York: Arno Press and The New York Times, 1968; reprint, New York: G.P. Putnam's Sons, 1883), 1: 61-68.

6. *Ibid.*, 68-69.

7. Tappan, *Arthur Tappan*, 136.

8. R. J. M. Blackett, "Anglo-American Opposition in Liberian Colonization, 1831-1833," *The Historian* 41 (February 1979): 277-279.

9. Nathan Irvin Huggins, *Slave and Citizen: The Life of Frederick Douglass* (Boston: Little Brown, and Company, 1980), 55, 178: Mehlinger, "Attitude of the Free Blacks," 295; Sorin, *Abolitionism*, 99-119; *Black Abolitionist Papers*, Introduction , 4-69; Garrison, *Thoughts on African Colonization*, part 2, 1-76.

10. *The American Convention of Abolition Societies, 1749-1829* (New York: Bergman Publishers, 1969), 1: 1-30.

11. Wendell Phillips Garrison and Francis Jackson Garrison, *William Lloyd Garrison, 1805-1879* (New York: Arno Press and The New York Times, 1969; reprint, New York: Century Co., 1885), 124-137.

12. Russel B. Nye, *William Lloyd Garrison and the Humanitarian Reformers* (Boston: Little Brown and Company, 1955), 24-27; Walter M. Merrill, *Against Wind and Tide: A Biography of Wm. Lloyd Garrison* (Cambridge: Harvard University Press, 1963), 30.

13. "To the Patrons of This Work," *Genius of the Universal Emancipation*, 10 (March 5, 1830): 205.

14. *Ibid.*

15. William Lloyd Garrison, *Thoughts on African Colonization* (New York: Arno Press and The New York Press, 1968; reprint, Boston: Garrison and Knapp, 1832), 1: 103-104.

16. Walters, *Antislavery Appeal*, 38, 41-42, 46.

17. James Gillespie Birney, *The American Churches: The Bulwarks of American Slavery* (New York: Arno Press and The New York Times: 1969;

reprint, Newburyport: Charles Whipple, 1842), 1-44. Sorin, *Abolitionism,* 48-52; Merton L. Dillon, *The Abolitionists: The Growth in a Dissenting Minority* (De Kalb: Northern Illinois University Press, 1974), 60.

18. "To The Public," *Liberator,* 1 (January 1, 1831): 1.

19. "Be Not Deceived!" *Liberator,* 1 (July 9, 1832): 109; Staudenraus claimed that Garrison "spent ten times more space on anti-colonization than on immediate emancipation" Staudenraus, *African Colonization,* 194.

20. Garrison, *African Colonization,* 11.

21. *Ibid.,* 12, 23.

22. *Ibid.,* 56.

23. *Ibid.,* 79-80.

24. *Ibid.,* 105.

25. *Ibid.,* 20-21.

26. Leonard L. Richards, *Gentlemen of Property and Standing: Anti-Abolition Mobs in Jacksonian America* (New York: Oxford University Press, 1970), 5, 23-30, 169.

27. Staudenraus, *African Colonization,* 214-215.

28. *Ibid.,* 201.

29. Arthur Tappan to Lewis F. Laine, March 26, 1833, in Lewis Tappan, *The Life of Arthur Tappan* (Westport: Negro Universities Press, 1970; reprint, New York: Hurd and Houghton, 1871), 128-130.

30. Wendell Philips Garrison, *William Garrison,* 1: 312.

31. Lewis, *Arthur Tappan,* 168-175.

32. Theodore D. Weld to Birney, September 27, 1832, in *Letters of James Gillespie Birney, 1831-1857,* Dwight L. Dumond, ed. (Gloucester: Peter Smith, 1966), 1: 27.

33. Robert H. Abzug, *Passionate Liberator: Theodore Dwight Weld and the Dilemma of Reform* (New York: Oxford University Press, 1980), 86-87. Benjamin P. Thomas, *Theodore Weld: Crusader for Freedom* (New Brunswick: Rutgers University Press, 1950), 35-37.

34. Theodore D. Weld to Birney, June 17, 1834, in *Letters of James Gillespie Birney,* 1: 116.

35. Abzug, *Passionate Liberator,* 89-94, 117-118, 120-122.

36. Ralph R. Gurley to Birney, June 12, July 7, and August 23, 1832, in *Letters to James Gillespie Birney,* 1: 5-8, 20-23.

37. "Colonization of the Free Colored People," *African Repository* 9 (August 1833): 172-174; 207-208; 239-240; 274-276; 311-313; 342-344.

38. Birney to Gerrit Smith, November 15, 1834, *Letters of James Gillespie Birney,* 1: 147-152.

39. James G. Birney to Weld, July 17, 1834, in *Letters of Theodore Dwight Weld, Angelina Grimke Weld, and Sarah Grimke, 1824-1844,* Gilbert H. Barnes and Dwight L. Dumond, eds. (New York: Da Capo Press, 1970), 1: 156-160.

40. Fox, *American Colonization Society*, 62; "Proceedings at the Seventeenth Annual Meeting of the American Colonization Society," *African Repository*, 9 (February 1834): 364.

41. Aileen S. Kraditor, *Means and Ends in American Abolitionism: Garrison and His Critics on Strategy and Tactics, 1834-1850* (New York: Pantheon Books, 1967), 242; Ronald Walters, *The Antislavery Appeal: American Abolitionism After 1830* (Baltimore: John Hopkins University Press, 1976), xiii, 23; Louis Filler, *The Crusade Against Slavery, 1830-1860* (New York: Harper and Row, 1960), 22.

42. "Speech of Mr. Clay, On the Subject of Abolition Petitions, in Senate, Thursday, February 7, 1839." *African Repository* 15 (February 1839): 50-64.

43. "Speech of Harrison Gray Otis," *African Repository* 11 (October 1835): 311-318.

44. William W. Freehling argued that the nullification crisis created by South Carolina was more than just a reaction to economic stress created by the Tariff of 1828 and 1832: "the nullification impulse was to a critical extent a revealing expression of South Carolina's morbid sensitivity to the beginnings of the antislavery campaign." William W. Freehling, *Prelude to Civil War: The Nullification Controversy in South Carolina, 1826-1836* (New York: Harper Torchbooks, 1965), x.

45. "Report Upon Abolition, Wednesday, May 18, 1836, in Gales and Seaton's," *Register of Debates in Congress* (14 vols., Washington: Gales and Seaton, 1824-1837), 12: 3756-1763, 4050-4055.

46. *Ibid.*

47. Proposed resolution in public land sales, February 28, 1825, *Register of Debates*, 1: 624; 696-697.

48. Address of Robert Y. Hayne, February 7, 1827, *Register of Debates*, 3: 289-296; 318-334.

49. Brutus (pseudo,. Robert James Turnball), *Essays on the Usurpations of the Federal Government* (Charleston: A. E. Miller, 1827), 89, 109-110, 124.

50. See chapter 2 for a fuller discussion of the revived interest in colonization sentiments as the sectional animosities increased.

51. "Early Antislavery Movement," 191.

Conclusion

The American Colonization Society, founded in 1817, aimed at removing free blacks from the United States to the western coast of Africa.
There it was assumed they would have a better life than in the land of
their birth while at the same time bringing Christianity and civilization to
the Dark Continent. This deportation of free blacks and later emancipated slaves was designed to alleviate the fears of race wars that southerners anticipated, should large numbers of slaves be immediately released. The American Colonization Society lobbied Congress to shape
African colonization into a national policy, but the scheme never received congressional endorsement. As an alternative to government action, the colonizationists turned to building state and local societies
across the United States as a means of raising funds and publicizing their
program. Ralph R. Gurley, secretary of the Society and editor of its official organ, the *African Repository,* forged colonization into a national
movement as colonizationists took the lead in the antislavery movement
during the 1820s. But they lost ground in the 1830s and 1840s to the
growing militant abolitionist movement which had no colonization
thrust.

The American Colonization Society failed in both its initial goal of
colonizing free blacks and in its later efforts to encourage voluntary and
gradual emancipation. The number of free blacks and emancipated slaves
transported to Africa was small when compared to the total number of
blacks in America.[1] The Society proved unable both to persuade a sig-
nificant body of free blacks that their happiest future lay in Africa and to
encourage a large number of slaveholders to emancipate their slaves.

Several major obstacles hindered the Society in accomplishing its
aims. First, the tremendous expenses for transporting and resettling im-

migrants in Africa rendered colonization impractical. The national Society along with the state and local auxiliaries simply could not raise the money required to undertake such a vast program as the effort failed to stir the general public to dynamic action. Too few whites in the North were seriously enough concerned about slavery to expend the economic and political capital which emancipation and colonization demanded. Between 1820 and 1860 fewer than 11,000 blacks immigrated to Africa. But since the 1860 census placed the slave population at 3,953,760 and the free black population at 488,000, the cost of transporting all slaves and free blacks would have been prohibitive.[2]

Second, since the slave trade had ended in 1807, almost all free blacks were born in the United States and were unwilling recruits for any colonization scheme. Several generations removed from Africa, they, of course, considered the United States their home and wished only to improve their condition in their native land. Only by armed force could full colonization have been effected, and this possibility did not exist.

Beyond this, the abolition movement also highlighted the inherent contradictions of the colonization program. Supporters of the colonization movement, convinced that white American's racial attitudes toward blacks could never be changed, opposed any legislation giving free blacks the right to vote and supported racial restrictions. According to colonizationists, resettling free blacks outside the United States proved both humane and just. Yet free blacks and radical abolitionists insisted that African colonization's propaganda describing blacks as inferior and incapable of citizenship only increased racial prejudice and hatred. Instead of the movement elevating free blacks, it actually lowered the status of free blacks.[3] Abolitionists, in addition, viewed the Society as a mechanism to rid the South of free blacks which reflected the almost universal fear among slave holders that free blacks posed a constant threat by helping fugitive slaves and provoking slave revolts.[4] They asserted that gradual emancipation combined with colonization actually hindered emancipation by alleviating slaveholders' moral uncertainties concerning slavery, thus strengthening the "peculiar institution." In the 1830s and 1840s abolitionists seized the lead in the antislavery movement from the colonizationists, and many early key advocates of colonization abandoned gradualism and adopted immediatism.

Finally, colonizationists could not interest the Deep South in the program, and this stronghold of slavery was critical to the Society's success. The Industrial Revolution and Eli Whitney's gin had made cotton production extraordinarily profitable for the South, and unprecedented levels of wealth hinged upon a large slave labor force. White southerners convinced themselves that their economic bonanza rested upon black slaves who could work in the fields in the lower South where white laborers might not work under such tropical conditions and, more saliently, could leave when they wished. In the end, they cared too deeply about the prosperity and social structure engendered by their "peculiar institution" to see it fundamentally shaken.

Although the American Colonization Society failed in accomplishing its goals, it did serve to bring about certain positive influences. The Society focused renewed attention on the illegal, but still active, slave trade. Colonizationists lobbied Congress to pass the Slave Trade Act in 1819 which authorized the president to take whatever action necessary to halt the international slave trade, particularly active along the coast of the Deep South. In addition, the colony established by the Society on Africa's western coast of Africa also effectively discouraged slave traffic that formerly had thrived in that region.

Yet another positive impact of the Society was to serve as a focal point for the antislavery movement, certainly in its early years. Its program implicitly indicted slavery and at the same time publicized the oppression of free blacks in northern cities. Many leaders in the abolitionist movement such as Theodore Weld and James Birney emerged from the ranks of the American Colonization Society and sharpened their skills that they would apply so dramatically in their later careers. Of course the proudest achievement of the colonization movement was the establishment of Liberia, the oldest republic in Africa.

After the Civil War the American Colonization Society continued functioning as an agency for promoting African-American immigration and education. Between 1861 and 1899, 4,869 African-Americans migrated to Liberia under its auspices, and with its contributions peaking at $160,303.23 in 1859, the Society constructed a four-story building on Pennsylvania Avenue in Washington D.C. The aging and eventual demise of the organization's original members, however, accelerated the Society's decline in the late nineteenth century. Marking the end of the Society's viability, the *African Repository* published its last volume in 1892.

Since the mid-nineteenth century the American civilization has fathered a variety of "back to Africa" movements, but the Colonization Society's failure points ineluctably to the conclusion that the answer to racial problems is not the separation of blacks and whites. Any solution to America's race problem lies in the races learning to live together as the abolitionists so tirelessly insisted. America's heritage demands such a resolution. Those crusaders of the American Colonization Society badly misread their people and culture. However noble or base their motives, they failed in the end to proffer a plan acceptable to either the masters of society or to those so wickedly oppressed. Although the movement's supporters rigorously pursued humanitarian goals, the Society floundered, failing to adequately address the existence of slavery in a society still experimenting with democracy.

NOTES

1. According to Staudenraus, between 1820 and 1860 some 10,517 blacks immigrated to Liberia. The total number of immigrants from 1820 to 1899 was 15,386. Staudenraus, *African Colonization*, 251; Lowenkopf claimed that about 22,000 immigrants were transported to Liberia. Lowenkopf further breaks down the types of Liberian immigrants: emancipated American slaves – 5,957; recaptured Africans – 5,722; free born American blacks – 4,541; free American blacks settled by the Maryland Colonization Society – 1,227; other emancipated American slaves – 753; West Indians – 346; American slaves who purchased their freedom – 344; and others – 68. Lowenkopf, *Politics in Liberia*, 14-16.

2. Samuel L. Rogers, *Negro Population in the United States, 1790-1915* (New York: Arno Press and The New York Times, 1968; reprint, Washington: Government Printing Office, 1918), 57.

3. Litwack, *North of Slavery*, 24-27.

4. Bancroft, "Early Antislavery Movement, 157-166.

BIBLIOGRAPHY

Primary Sources

The African Repository and Colonial Journal. 68 vols. Washington: American Colonization Society, 1825-1894.

The American Convention of Abolition Societies, 1789-1829. 3 vols. New York: Bergman Publishers, 1969.

Brutus [Robert Turnbull]. *Essays of the Usurpations of the Federal Government.* Charles: A. E.Miller, 1827.

Daily National Intelligencer. Vols. 4-5.

Debates and Proceedings of the Congress of the United States, 1789-1824: Annals of the Congress of the United States. 42 vols. Washington: Gates and Seaton, 1834-1856.

Garrison, William Lloyd. *Thoughts on African Colonization.* New York: Arno Press and *The New York Times*, 1968; reprint, Boston: Garrison and Knapp, 1832.

Genius of Universal Emancipation. Benjamin Lundy, ed., 1830, Vol. 10.

The Liberator. William Lloyd Garrison, ed., 1831, Vol. 1.

Register of Debates in Congress. 14 vols. Washington: Gales and Seaton, 1825-1837.

Tappan, Lewis. *The Life of Arthur Tappan.* New York: Hurd and Houghton; reprint, Westpoint: Negro Universities Press, 1970.

Secondary Sources

Abzug, Robert H. *Passionate Liberator: Theodore Dwight Weld and the Dilemma of Reform*. New York: Oxford University Press, 1980.

Adams, Charles Francis, ed. *Memoirs of John Quincy Adams, Comprising Portions of His Diary From 1785 to 1848*. Philadelphia: J. B. Tippinott, 1875.

Alexander, Archibald. *A History of Colonization on the Western Coast of Africa*. 2d. ed. Freeport: Books for Libraries Press, 1971; reprint, Philadelphia: William S. Martien, 1849.

Ames, Herman V. *State Documents on Federal Relations: The States and the United States*. New York: Da Capo Press, 1970.

Ammon, Harry. *James Monroe: The Quest for National Identity*. New York: McGraw-Hill Book Company, 1971.

Ashmun, J. *History of the African Colony in Liberia, From December 1821 to 1823*. Washington: Way and Gideon, 1826.

Bancroft, Frederic, "The Early Antislavery Movement and African Colonization," in *Frederic Bancroft, Historian: With an Introduction by Allan Nevins and Three Hitherto Un-published Essays on the Essays on the Colonization of American Negroes from 1801 to 1865 by Frederic Bancroft*. ed. Jacob E. Cooke, 147-191. Norman: University of Oklahoma Press, 1957.

Barnes, Gilbert H. and Dwight L. Dummond, eds. *Letters of Theodore Dwight Weld, Angelina Grimke Weld, and Sarah Grimke, 1822-1844*. 2 vols. New York: Da Capo Press, 1970.

Basler, Roy P. *The Collected Works of Abraham Lincoln. 4 vols*. New Brunswick: New Jersey, 1953.

Bergh, Albert Ellegry, ed. *The Writings of Jefferson*. 20 vols. Washington: The Thomas Jefferson Memorial Association, 1905.

Birney, James Gillespie. *The American Churches: The Bulwarks of American Slavery* New York: Arno Press and The New York

Blackett, R. J. M. "Anglo-American Opposition to Liberian Colonization, 1831-1833." *Historian.* 41 (February 1979): 276-294.

Brant, Irving. *James Madison: Commander in Chief, 1812-1836.* Indianapolis: The Bobbs-Merrill Company, 1961.

Brawley, Benjamin. *A Social History of the American Negro.* New York: The MacMillian Company, 1921.

Brown, Delindus R. "Free Blacks' Rhetorical Impact of African Colonization: The Emergence of Rhetorical Exigence." *Journal of Black Studies.* 3 (March 1979):151-165.

Brown, Isaac V. *Biography of the Rev. Robert Finley.* Philadelphia: John W. Moore, 1857; reprint, New York: Arno Press and The New York Times, 1969.

Cresson, W.P. *James Monroe.* Chapel Hill: University of North Carolina Press, 1946.

Dangerfield, George. *The Awakening of American Nationalism, 1815-1818.* New York: Harper and Row, 1965.

Dawidoff, Robert. *The Education of John Randolph.* New York: W. W. Norton, 1979.

Deusen, Glyndon G. Van. *The Life of Henry Clay.* Boston: Little, Brown, and Company, 1937.

Dillon, Merton L. *The Abolitionist: The Growth of a Dissenting Minority.* De Kald: Northern Illinois University Press, 1974.

Dumond, Dwight L., ed. *Letters of James Gillespie Birney, 1831-1857.* 12 vols.Gloucester: Peter Smith, 1966.

Eaton, Clement. *Henry Clay and the Art of American Politics.* Boston: Little, Brown, and Company, 1957.

Filler, Louis. *The Crusade against Slavery 1830-1860.* New York:

Fogel, Robert William. *Without Consent or Contract: the Rise and Fall of American Slavery*. New York: W. W. Norton and Company, 1989.

Ford, Paul Leicester, ed. *The Writings of Jefferson*. 10 vols. New York: G. P.Putnam's Sons, 1889.

Fox, Early Lee. *The American Colonization Society, 1817-1840*. Baltimore: John Hopkins Press, 1919.

Freehling, William W. *Prelude to Civil War: The Nullification Controversy in South Carolina, 1816-1836*. New York: Harper and Row, 1965, 1966.

Garrison, Wendell Phillips and Francis Jackson Garrison. *William Lloyd Garrison, 1805-1879*. New York: Arno Press and The New York Times, 1969; reprint, New York: Century Co., 1885.

Gershoni, Yekutiel. *Black Colonization: The Americo-Liberian Scramble for the Hinterland*. Boulder: Westview Press, 1985.

Green, Constance McL. *Eli Whitney and the Birth of American Technology*. Glenview: Little, Brown, and Company, 1956.

Gross, Bella. "The First National Negro Convention." *The Journal of Negro History*. 31 (October 1946): 435-443.

Gurley, Ralph Randolph. *Life of Jehudi Ashmun, Late Colonial Agent in Liberia*. Freeport: Books for Libraries Press, 1971 (1835).

Hamilton, Stanislaus Murry, ed. *The Writings of James Monroe*. 6 vols. New York: G. P. Putman's Sons, 1900.

Handlin, Oscar and Mary F. "Origins of the Southern Labor System." *William and Mary Quarterly*. 7 (April 1950): 199-222.

Hopkins, James F., ed. *The Papers of Henry Clay*. 9 vols. Lexington: University of Kentucky, 1961.

Howe, Daniel Walker. *The Political Culture of the American Whigs*. Chicago: The University of Chicago Press, 1979

Huggins, Nathan Irvin. *Slave and Citizen: The Life of Frederick Douglass*. Boston: Little, Brown, and Company, 1980.

Jordan, Winthrop D. *White over Black: American Attitudes towards the Negro, 1550-1812*. Chapel Hill: University of North Carolina Press, 1918.

Kraditor, Aileen S. *Means and Ends in American Abolitionism: Garrison and His Critics on Strategy and Tactics, 1834-1850*. New York: Pantheon Books, 1967.

Kupp, A. P. *Sierra Leone: A Concise History*. New York: St. Martin's Press, 1785.

Litwack, Leon F. *North of Slavery: The Negro in the Free States, 1790-1860*. Chicago: The University of Chicago, 1961.

Locke, Mary Stoughton. *Anti-Slavery in America from the Introduction of African Slaves to the Prohibition of the Slave Trade, 1619-1808*. Radcliffe College, 1901; reprint, Gloucester: Peter Smith, 1965.

Lowenkopf, Martin. *Politics in Liberia: The Conservative Road to Development*. Stanford: Hoover Institution Press, 1976.

Matijastic, Thomas D. "Whig Support for African Colonization: Ohio as a Test Case." *Mid-America: A Historical Review*. 66 (April-July 1984): 79-91.

McCoy, Drew R. *The Last of the Fathers: James Madison and the Republican Legacy*. Cambridge: Cambridge University Press, 1989.

McMaster, John Back. *A History of the People of the United States*. 8 vols. New York: D. Appleton-Century Company, 1938 (1883, 1911).

Mehlinger, Louis R. "The Attitude of the Free Negro toward African Colonization." *The Journal of Negro History* 1 (July 1916): 276-301.

Mellon, Matthew T., ed. *Early American Views on Negro Slavery: From the Letters and Papers of the Founders of the Republic.* New York: Bergman Publishers, 1969.

Merrill, Walters M. *Against Wind and Tide: A Biography of Wm. Lloyd Garrison.* Cambridge: Harvard University Press, 1963.

Nye, Russel B. *William Lloyd Garrison and the Humanitarian Reformers.* Boston: Little, Brown, and Company, 1955.

Perry, Lewis and Michael Fellman. *Antislavery Reconsidered: New Perspectives on the Abolitionists.* Baton Rouge: Louisiana State University, 1979.

Pessen, Edward, *Jacksonian America: Society, Personality, and Politics.* Urbana: University of Illinois Press, 1985.

Peterson, John. *Province of Freedom: A History of Sierra Leone, 1789-1870.* Evanston: Northwestern University Press, 1969.

Peterson, Merrill D., ed. *The Portable Thomas Jefferson.* New York: Penguin Books, 1977.

Rayback, Robert J. *Millard Fillmore: Biography of a President.* Buffalo: Henry Steward, 1959.

Remini, Robert V., *The Revolutionary Age of Andrew Jackson.* New York: Harper & Row, 1987.

Richards, James D. *A Compilation of the Messages and Papers of the Presidents.* 20 Vols. New York: Bureau of National Literature, 1897.

Richards, Leonard L. *"Gentlemen of Property and Standing:" Anti-Abolition Mobs in Jacksonian America.* New York: Oxford University Press, 1970.

Ripley, C. Peter, ed. *The Abolitionist Papers.* 4 vols. Chapel Hill: University of North Carolina Press, 1991.

Rogers, Samuel L. *Negro Population in the United States, 1790-1915*. New York: Arno Press and *The New York Times*, 1968; reprint, Washington: Government Printing Office, 1918.

Schurz, Carl. *Henry Clay*. 2 vols. 1915; reprint, New York: Frederich Ungar Publishing, 1968.

Sherwood, N. H. "Early Negro Deportation Projects." *Mississippi Valley Historical Review*. 2 (March 1916): 484-508.

Smelser, Marshal. *The Democratic Republic, 1801-1815*. New York: Harper and Row, 1968.

Sorin, Gerald. *Abolitionism: A New Perspective*. New York: Praeger Publishers, 1972.

Staudenraus, P. J. *The African Colonization Movement, 1816-1865*. New York: Columbia University Press, 1961.

Streifford, David M. "The American Colonization Society: An Application of Republican Ideology to Early Antebellum Reform." *Journal of Southern History*. 45 (May 1979): 201- 220.

Sweet, Leonard I. *Black Images of America, 1864-1870*. New York: W. W. Norton and Company, 1976.

Thomas, Benjamin P. *Theodore Weld: Crusader for Freedom*. New Brunswick: Rutgers University Press, 1950.

Utting, A. J. *The Story of Sierra Leone*. Hallandale: New World Book Manufacturing, 1931; reprint, Freeport: Books for Libraries Press, 1971.

Walker, James W. St. G. *The Black Loyalists: The Search for a Promised Land in Nova Scotia and Sierra Leone, 1783-1870*. New York: Africana Publishing Company and Dalhousie University Press, 1976.

Walters, Ronald G. *The Antislavery Appeal: American Abolitionism After 1830*. Baltimore: The John Hopkins University Press, 1976.

Webster, Daniel. *The Writings and Speeches of Daniel Webster*. 18 vols.

Welch, Galbraith. *The Jet Lighthouse*. London: Museum Press Limited, 1960.

West, Richard. *Back to Africa: A History of Sierra Leone and Liberia*. London: Jonathan Cape, 1970.

Williams, George W. *History of the Negro Race in America, 1619-1880: Negroes as Slaves, as Soldiers, and as Citizens*.

Wilson, Charles Morrow. *Liberia*. New York: William Sloanne Associates, 1947.

Wilson, Charles Morrow. *Liberia: Black Africa in Microcosm*. New York: Harper and Row, 1971.

Woodson, Carter ed. "Transplanting Free Negroes to Ohio from 1815 to 1858." *The Journal of Negro History*. 1 (July 1916): 302-317.

Index

Allan Yarema is an assistant professor in the department of history at Abilene Christian University. He was born and raised in Dauphin, Manitoba, Canada. After marrying a "southern belle" from Louisiana, they decided to live between Louisiana and Canada. They ended up in Texas where he earned a BA in history, BS in political science, and an EdD with a minor in history from Texas A & M University – Commerce. While working on his degrees he was employed as a teaching assistant in the history department as well as an assistant instructor at Northeast Texas Community College where he taught both American history survey and government courses. He also earned a MAG degree in geography from Texas State University. In addition to American survey courses, he currently teaches History for Teachers, World Geography, and Cultural Geography. He is also the advisor for students seeking history and social studies state certification. He has enjoyed life with his "southern belle" who also teaches in the Mathematics and Computer Science department at Abilene Christian University.